Hawai'i

A Pictorial Celebration

by Ellie Crowe

Photography by Elan Penn

Sterling Publishing Co., Inc.
New York

Designed by Michel Opatowski
Edited by J. E. Sigler
Layout by Gala Pre Press Ltd.

Many people have graciously contributed their time, knowledge, and expertise to this book. The author would like to give special thanks to the following: Rubellite Kawena Johnson, emerita professor of Hawaiian Language and Literature, University of Hawai'i at Mānoa; Martha Yent, Archaeology and Interpretive Programs Division of State Parks, Department of Lands and Natural Resources; Dr. Yoshiko Sinoto, Senior Anthropologist, and the staff of the Bishop Museum; photographer William Crowe; archivists at the Hawai'i State Archives; librarians at the Hawai'i State Library and the Hawai'i Kai and Aina Haina Libraries; park rangers of the National Parks Service; Chipper Wichman, Director of Kahanu Gardens; Professor David Saunders, University of Hawai'i Observatory on Mauna Kea; Patrick McLain, Director of Operations and dolphin expert at Dolphin Quest Hawai'i; Leanne Pletcher, Marketing Manager, and Debbie Hogan, Director of Sales, Hilton Waikoloa Village; Aven Wright-McIntosh, Director of Public Relations, Mauna Kea Resort; Ric Elhard, owner of Kula Kai Caverns; Victor Lozano of Hawai'i Dolphin and Whale Watching Tours; Linda Beech, Waipi'o Valley; Thomas O. Plant, Chief Inspector on the H-3 Interstate; military veterans and navy personnel at the USS Arizona Memorial and USS Missouri; Sean Connell, wind surfing expert at Naish Hawai'i in Kailua; John Morgan of Kualoa Ranch; paniolo at Parker Ranch; and Dr. Robert Tyson, movie buff. I am also grateful to fellow writers and/or island-seekers Juliet and Aaron Fry, Caroline Bennet, Ron Bessems, Adam Crowe, Jim and Sandy Rodin, Elizabeth Womersley, Lynne Wikoff, Tammy Yee, Elaine Masters, Sue Cowing, Nancy Mower, Susan Morrison, and Marion Coste.

I dedicate this book to my expert critics: Will, Juliet, Caroline, and Adam, and to excellent Penn Publishing editor Jennifer Sigler.

The lovely flower leis were found at Cindy's Leis, Chinatown, Honolulu. Penn Publishing gratefully acknowledges the following institutions and individuals for allowing photographs from their collections to be reproduced in this book:

Hawai'i State Archives 7, 8,9, 10-11, 12-13, 14, 15, 16, 17, 18, 19, 20, 21, 22, 23, 24, 25
Hawai'i Visitors & Convention Bureau 1, 28, 32, 40, 57, 58, 60, 61, 78, 79, 122, 124, 126, 128, 134, 135, 159
Ken Ige, Star-Bulletin 115
William Crowe 1, 34, 56, 64, 71, 72, 73, 114, 121, 150

Library of Congress Cataloging in Publication data is available from the Publisher

2 4 6 8 10 9 7 5 3 1

Published by Sterling Publishing Co., Inc.
387 Park Avenue South, New York, NY 10016
Copyright © 2006 by Penn Publishing Ltd.
Distributed in Canada by Sterling Publishing
c/o Canadian Manda Group, 165 Dufferin Street,
Toronto, Ontario, Canada M6K 3H6
Distributed in the United Kingdom by GMC Distribution Services,
Castle Place, 166 High Street, Lewes, East Sussex, England BN7 1XU
Distributed in Australia by Capricorn Link (Australia) Pty. Ltd.
P.O. Box 704, Windsor, NSW 2756, Australia

Sterling ISBN-13:978-1-4027-2407-7
ISBN-10:1-4027-2407-1

For information about custom editions, special sales, premium and corporate purchases, please contact Sterling Special Sales Department at 800-805-5489 or specialsales@sterlingpub.com.

Opposite: Sunset at Keawakapu Beach, Maui

Contents

Foreword by Professor Rubellite Kawena Kinney Johnson

Professor Emerita Rubellite Kawena Kinney Johnson is considered by many the leading scholar on Hawai'i today. Throughout her long career as professor at the University of Hawai'i, she has contributed to the academic record a virtual treasure trove of distinguished research on Hawaiian and Polynesian language, literature, history, archaeology, and culture. In 1983, the Honpa Hongwanji Mission of Hawai'i designated her a "Living Treasure of Hawai'i."

In addition, Professor Johnson is one of the few native Hawaiians who can trace their descendancy directly to the great King Kamehameha. This lineage has not only endeared her to the residents of these islands as a living symbol of their rich heritage and traditions, but also gives her unique insight into the history and culture of her land. She has recommended two of this author's other works on Hawai'i. Both publisher and author would like to thank her for graciously reviewing this work as well.

Once again, Ellie Crowe has managed to reveal simply and enjoyably the many faces of Hawai'i in all their historical and mystical complexity. Through descriptions of her own crafting, Elan Penn's breathtaking images of places of interest, the mysterious refrains of ancient Hawaiian chants and songs, and the inspiring words of immigrants and visitors to the islands, she has woven a truly faithful tale of this land from the very same colorful threads found within its cultural and social tapestry.

There is not a single place along this geographic journey through hill- and mountain-sides, jungle valleys, volcanoes above and under the sea, ocean surfs, temple grounds, and historic buildings in which she does not invoke the love of the Hawaiian people for this land. In these places are captured the cultures, religions, languages, even the personal tragedies and triumphs of those who lived, loved, and died here. Of those whose ancestors sailed from far-away Polynesia to make this fabled land romantic with their tales of love and dramatic with their adventures in war, she tells with the same passion and nostalgia felt by their own descendants still alive today. Of those whose forebears immigrated hither, whose vision and dedication have dotted our wild landscapes with great metropolises, she tells with the same adoration and wonder that visitors still feel upon arriving in this bewildering land of contrasts.

These geographies, histories, peoples, and cultures have mixed to create in Hawai'i a cosmopolitan society both hauntingly ancient and spectacularly modern. With great success, Ellie skillfully balances these stories of honored heritage and welcome change, natural reverence and human practicality, and indigenous familiarity and foreign interest. It is a balance which gives *The Islands of Hawai'i* the same intense feeling that permeates the very air of Hawai'i: that all who come here, whether to visit or to make their home, *belong* here. That is the very meaning of Hawaiian *aloha*, "love." That is the way it has always been—and may it always be so.

As we travel through these awe-inspiring landscapes and breathe in the powerful memories of these magnificent peoples, let us remember that you and I are their inheritors: children of the same earth under the same sky, watching the same ocean from sunrise to sunset beneath the same swaying palms of these islands. So, also, do we sing the same song:

Goodbye, may God bless you wherever you may go, It's a long time to say *aloha*, for you'll never find another *kanaka* [people] like me, Oh no, you'll never find another *kanaka* like me.

—Rubellite Kawena Kinney Johnson

The Hawaiian Islands: Land of Legends, Love, and

No alien land in all the world has any deep strong charm for me but that one, no other land could so longingly and so beseechingly haunt me, sleeping and waking, through half a lifetime, as that one has done. Other things leave me, but it abides; other things change, but it remains the same.

—Mark Twain

Since the beginning, when steam clouds swirled across the sky and the first fountain of fire-red lava burst from the Pacific Ocean, the Islands of Hawai'i have represented Nature at her most extravagant. Their extraordinary physical beauty draws millions of visitors every year, and the culture and heritage of the local people convince many of them to stay. Hawai'i is a melting pot of East and West, where each culture retains its own identity even as it blends with the others for mutual enrichment. Most fascinating are the history, legends, and myths of the host culture, the Hawaiians, whose ancestors left a legacy of extraordinary richness that enhances every part of life in the islands today. Visiting in the first half of the twentieth century, world traveler and writer Somerset Maugham sensed these deep, almost mystical roots: "Though the air is so soft and the sky is so blue, you have, I know not why, a feeling of something hotly passionate that beats like a throbbing pulse through the crowd . . . a little below there is a darkness and mystery."

This pictorial journey through the islands visits the beautiful locations frequented by visitors today, revealing the history, mystery, and magic that dwell just beneath the surface of these beloved sites. To start the adventure off right, one must begin where the Hawaiians did, with the Hawaiian creation chant called the *Kumulipo*, which begins: *At the time when the earth became hot...*

Praise to Pele: The Volcanoes

The Hawaiian Islands were conceived by fire when, about 80 million years ago, in the dark depths 16,500 feet below sea level, a crack

Hawaiian chief, circa 1779

A kapu breaker (transgressor of sacred law) is strangled to death, circa 1779.

developed in the ocean floor and incandescent magma gushed from the interior of the earth. As eruption after eruption shook the ocean, successive flows of red-hot lava merged with the cold seawater and hardened into a seamount. Thousands of years later, a volcanic peak broke through the surface of the sea—and an island was born! However, as an island grows and rises out of the sea, it gradually moves away from its hotspot, that mysterious crack in the ocean floor from which its life-giving lava flows. Once separated from its hotspot, a volcano dies, and the island starts to erode and sink back into the sea, leaving only a fringe of coral reef.

Luckily, this island life cycle is arduously slow. The 82 volcanoes that now comprise the back-bone of the Hawaiian Islands were formed over 44 million years from a single hotspot. There are eight major islands in the chain—Ni'ihau, Kaua'i, O'ahu, Moloka'i, Lāna'i, Maui, Kaho'olawe, and Hawai'i—as well as 1,600 miles of reefs, atolls, and shoals. The major islands are still major because they emerged last: The youngest island, the Big Island of Hawai'i, still has active volcanoes —Kīlauea and Mauna Loa can be visited at Hawai'i Volcanoes National Park—and is even still growing. The newest up-and-coming island, Lo'ihi Seamount, has tens of thousands of years to grow until it, too, bursts from the depths of the ocean. Other volcanoes, like Mauna Kea, Hualālei, and Haleakalā, are considered dormant. All the other volcanoes on the islands, like Diamond Head, are considered extinct.

Kapo's Kingdom: The Wildness and the Wet

At a distance of over 2,000 miles from any continental landfall, the Hawaiian Islands were a difficult place for most organisms to reach. Riding the waves and storm winds, seeds, spores, insects, and birds arrived one by one over millions of years. The few adventurous species that succeeded in reaching these distant shores evolved in unexpected ways, creating a profusion of life forms found nowhere else on earth. On these newborn islands there were no predators, so poisonous plants lost their poison, thorny raspberry bushes lost their thorns, and bitter tree bark became sweet. The insects and birds that made it to the islands are also examples of the "use it or lose it" concept: One little spider's dull coloring, which hid it from hungry predators back home, became bright yellow with red markings so similar to eyes and a smile that it is now named "the Happy-Face Spider"—pretty hard to miss! Some species of geese, ibis, rails, and honeycreepers lost their ability to fly, and non-threatened shearwaters started a dangerous prac-

tice of building nests on the ground. Finding plenty of space, sunshine, and water, plants and animals just relaxed and went with the old tropical island vibe, becoming less competitive for resources than their continental ancestors.

All the islands still have areas of unexplored wilderness. Visitors to the Big Island of Hawai'i can explore the remote Waipi'o Valley. The winding road to Hāna in East Maui leads to the unspoiled Ke'anae Peninsula, the caves and black sand beach of Wai'ānapanapa, and the beautiful Seven Sacred Pools of 'Ohe'o Gulch. Moloka'i's Hālawa Valley remains totally undeveloped. And

even busy O'ahu has unspoiled valleys like Kualoa Valley. The garden island of Kaua'i is home to an abundance of wild places: Waimea Canyon State Park in the west, the almost inaccessible Mount Wai'ale'ale in the center, and ravishingly beautiful valleys like Kalalau and Nu'alolo on the northern Nā Pali Coast.

For millions of years, the wild places of Hawai'i were uninhabited by human beings. Elsewhere, dynasties rose and fell; Caesars ruled; Christ, Buddha, Moses, and Mohammed preached. But Hawai'i, farther from any landmass than anyplace else on earth, remained untouched. And then, one day, the people came.

Fierce Chiefs and Feather Gods: Remnants of the Ancients

The presence of the ancient Hawaiians is etched in the Hawaiian landscape: in stone footpaths built through hidden valleys and across barren lava fields, and on high mountains where immense stone temples tell of gods and powerful chiefs. Under the cacophony of cities and bustling modern life, their ancient legends and myths echo like the throb of a gourd drum.

The very first settlers arrived around 500 A.D., probably in a canoe from the Marquesas Islands. Legends call them the Menehune, a peaceful people of small stature but extraordinary endurance. They left their mark on the islands with uniquely hewn rock walls, temples, pathways, ditches, and fishponds like the ʻAlekoko Menehune Fish Pond on Kauaʻi. Perhaps other Polynesian arrivals around this time were the stuff from which legends and gods are made: Maui, a sort of Polynesian superman, is said to have "pulled the islands out of the sea." Does that mean that he discovered them?

Around the twelfth century, a large wave of settlers arrived: powerful, warlike Tahitians in large double-hulled canoes similar to the *Hōkūleʻa*, a modern replica of an ancient Polynesian ocean-going canoe. Because ancient Hawaiʻi had no written history, the lengthy and numerous oral chants of the Tahitians, passed down through the ages, became the primary source of information about the islands' history. The chants relate that one of these new arrivals was Paʻao, a *powerful* kahuna (priest). The weak gods and the mellow lifestyle of Hawaiian chiefs—who were marrying commoners—appalled Paʻao, and he sent back to Tahiti for a powerful high chief, Pili, to help him set things right. They introduced powerful new gods, including Kū, the hungry god of war and human sacrifice, whose fierce carved image and snarling, feathered head can be seen in the Bishop Museum in Honolulu.

The Death of Captain Cook, 1779, by John Webber

Previous page: Hawaiian kāhuna wearing gourd masks meet Captain Cook's ship in 1779.

Above: High-ranking Hawaiian woman, as depicted by Louis Choris, 1816.

Because they traced their genealogies to the gods, the new chiefs possessed powerful *mana*, which they used to rule commoners with feudal power. To prevent their mana from being diluted, they married within the family: a high chief's marriage to his sister was a highly desirable union. The chiefs put the common people to work building immense luakini heiau, stone temples of war and human sacrifice, such as Pu'ukoholā Heiau on the Big Island of Hawai'i and Pi'ilanihale Heiau on Maui. Some temples were places of refuge, such as Pu'uhonua o Honaunau on the Big Island, where breakers of the sacred law could find shelter. Other temples were built to honor the various gods of agriculture, fishing, healing, and fertility.

Pa'ao introduced the *kapu*, sacred law, to protect the mana of the chiefs and to help maintain order. The *kapu* system governed all parts of ancient Hawaiian life, and though some laws were for the benefit of all (such as those that protected against over-planting and over-fishing), the majority were onerous for the common people (such as those that forbade women from eating certain foods). Breaking one of the laws had terrible consequences—angry gods caused volcanoes to erupt, tidal waves to flood the shores, and earthquakes to devastate the land—so *kapu* breakers had to be put to death and offered as human sacrifices at the heiau. This new religion did much to guarantee the power of the chiefs—there's nothing like a bit of human sacrifice to really get respect!

When not worrying about being sacrificed to deities, the Hawaiians of long ago had a superior capacity for enjoying themselves. The islands they'd discovered were welcoming and fertile, and the climate was perfect. Many gods were benevolent, and phallic rocks and fish gods abounded to assist devotees. When Hawaiians worked, they worked hard, but when their needs were met, they quit working. A person's worth was measured not by what he could accumulate,

Big Island, 1779

but by what he could give. Gifting was reciprocated, and the exchange of goods and services promoted the well-being of all.

During the annual four-month *makahiki* (harvest festival), the people had plenty of time to play and compete at games, wrestle, practice *lua* (a form of martial arts), compose lilting songs, and dance the hula at feasts and temples of hula, such as Ka-ulu-o-Laka Heiau on Kēʻē Beach. When the surf was up, whole villages would drop what they were doing and rush to the water with long surfboards. Fishing, too, was a greatly respected pastime.

With the *kapu* law in place and an elaborate system of rituals and cycle of festivals to keep people busy, life in ancient Hawaiʻi ran pretty predictably and smoothly. But everything was about to change. Everything.

Monarchs, Missionaries, and Moguls: The Western World Discovers Hawaiʻi

In 1778, the Hawaiians sighted strange objects on the horizon, like "trees moving on the sea." These floating islands with cloudlike sails anchored in Kealekekua Bay. *Kāhuna* regarded the pale-skinned seamen on the British ships as supernatural beings. Captain Cook, the world-famous British explorer, was hailed as the god Lono, returning as promised to his people.

At the time of Captain Cook's arrival, the

Honolulu, 1853

Hawaiian Islands were divided into four kingdoms, each ruled by power-hungry chiefs. Kalaniopu'u, chief of the Island of Hawai'i, is the one who greeted Captain Cook. Also present at this historic meeting on HMS *Resolution* was Kalaniopu'u's nephew, a young warrior by the name of Kamehameha. The ambitious Kamehameha noted the mighty magic of Western weapons, the cannons and the armaments, and just over a decade later he would use these tools to fulfill his royal destiny by conquering and uniting the islands under his rule.

For Captain Cook, too, destiny was running its course. The British seamen had landed in an earthly paradise filled with obliging Hawaiian women; the Hawaiian men, watching the sailors' enthusiastic gratification of their manly needs, began to suspect that the visitors were not in fact gods. Cook set sail, but a storm at sea forced the ships to return. On arriving again, the seamen found their welcome running out, and eventually a skirmish took place over a stolen rowboat. When Captain Cook was injured in the fray and bled to death from his wounds, it proved to the Hawaiians that he was in fact only human. With only a small parcel said to contain some of their beloved captain's bones, the shaken British seamen sailed away from the hostile islanders.

But for Hawai'i there was no going back. Western civilization had discovered the islands, and the Hawaiian people were about to be catapulted into the modern world. Beginning in late 1794, when the first British fur trading ship arrived at Honolulu, the promise of safe anchorage, fresh water, and food there and at Lahaina on Maui drew whalers, adventurers, sandalwood traders, sailors, and merchants from America and Europe. Astute Kamehameha I, now ruler of the entire island chain, gained knowledge of Western ways. He cooperated with the foreigners and encouraged industry and

trading, but he never allowed outsiders to buy land.

In May 1819, Kamehameha I died, and his favorite wife, Queen Ka'ahumanu, named herself Regent and shared the throne with Kamehameha's young heir, Liholiho. Kamehameha had held fast to the ancient religion, but the Hawaiians noted that the Western arrivals broke the sacred laws and suffered no consequences. The *kapu* law was harsh to women in particular, and the two powerful queens, Ka'ahumanu and Keōpūolani, seized this opportunity to abolish it. The ancient ceremonies were outlawed, and Liholiho ordered the heiau and idols destroyed.

Within six months, in one of history's oddest coincidences, New England missionaries sailed into this spiritual vacuum with a new God and a

Downtown Honolulu, 1874

17

Above: King Kalākaua, 1874

mission to convert the heathen savages. They acquired land from Kamehameha II and built the mission houses and Kawaiaha'o Church in Honolulu, Waiola Church in Lahaina, and the Wai'oli mission houses and church in Hanalei. They learned the Hawaiian language and created a written form of it for the first time in order to be able to translate the Bible into Hawaiian.

But despite the good the missionaries did, the Hawaiians were made to feel that their culture was inferior and needed to be improved. Abandonment of Hawaiian traditions and assimilation to Western ways spread like wildfire. To make matters worse, the native Hawaiian population was already dwindling by the 1850s: the sailors and whalers and other immigrants they had welcomed had brought to this isolated and disease-free Eden the deadly diseases of syphilis, gonorrhea, measles, influenza, tuberculosis, and smallpox, and had even created a dreaded leper colony at Kalaupapa.

Right: Honolulu Harbor, 1881

Kawaiahao Church, with Waikīkī and Diamond Head in background, 1887

Entrepreneurial traders who bought the islands' fragrant sandalwood brought money to the king and chiefs. But to the commoners, they brought only hard work. Foreigners began to farm the lands and control and breed huge herds of wild cattle, eventually establishing the immense Parker Ranch on the Big Island of Hawai'i. They invested enormous amounts of money and labor in the islands, and soon they wanted security for those investments. If they could not buy land, they threatened, they would leave and take their money with them. Under their pressure and the influence of his foreign counselors, Kamehameha III proclaimed the Great Mahele, a ruling that divided the land between the monarchy, the chiefs, and the commoners and gave foreigners the ability to buy land. Within thirty years, Westerners owned 80% of the islands' private land. By the late 1800s, huge tracts of land were consolidated into pineapple plantations on O'ahu and sugar

plantations on Kaua'i, O'ahu, and Maui. Laborers were brought in from Portugal and Asia to do the backbreaking work, thus adding more variety to the melting pot of Hawaiian society: Polynesian, Caucasian, and Oriental. Kamehameha IV encouraged commerce, agriculture, and the construction of schools, roads, and harbors. Hawai'i's economy prospered, but foreigners prospered far more than native Hawaiians. To the latter, enterprise was an entirely new idea—their language did not even have a word for merchant or trade.

The final blow to the way things were was soon struck. The great Kamehameha dynasty ended with the death of the last of its royal line, and King Kalākaua, the "Merrie Monarch," took the throne in 1874. He built 'Iolani Palace and did much to restore Hawaiian culture by recording ancient legends and bringing back the banned hula, but his regime was riddled with corruption and self-serving advisors. The political tension this caused came to a head when Kalākaua died in 1891 and his sister, Liliuʻokalani, became queen and tried to reclaim the powers of the monarchy. Businessmen and plantation owners, fearing once again for their investments, rallied for the annexation of Hawaiʻi to the democratic United States. In January 1893, the annexationists succeeded in a bloodless revolution to overthrow the Hawaiian monarchy. The following year, Sanford B. Dole, head of Hawaiʻi's Supreme Court, became president of the provisional government. Four years later, U.S. President McKinley signed the annexation agreement, making Hawaiʻi a territory of the United States.

America's Island Stronghold: Military Memories and Muscle

American financial interests in the Hawaiian Islands were now secured and could continue to grow uninhibited. The U.S. Government was among the first of the new prospectors, noting Hawaiʻi's strategic location right in the middle of the Pacific Ocean. During the Spanish-American War, U.S. troops were billeted at the foot of Diamond Head, and Schofield Barracks received the 5th Calvary in 1909. Soon, a huge navy base was established at Pearl Harbor, increasing the new territory's military importance exponentially.

The Japanese attack on Pearl Harbor was the pivotal event that drew America into World War II. Two mighty battleships, the sunken USS *Arizona* and the USS *Missouri* in Pearl Harbor, are reminders of this terrible war and the toll it took. The USS Arizona Memorial and the National Memorial Cemetery of the Pacific at Punchbowl are Hawaiʻi's two most visited sites, where residents and travelers pay their respects to those who gave their lives for the freedom of their fellow men.

Today, Hawaiʻi holds the single largest United States military presence in the world.

Waikīkī Moana Hotel, with Diamond Head in background, 1913

The headquarters of CINPAC (Commander in Chief, U.S. Pacific Command) in Oʻahu controls all the country's military activities in both the Pacific and Indian Oceans, an area of more than 100 million square miles extending from the U.S. West Coast to the eastern coast of Africa and including 43 nations—an awesome responsibility! All branches of the military are represented on bases around Oʻahu, military ships cruise offshore, military aircraft streak through the skies, and military personnel make up a significant percentage of Hawaiʻi's population. These and other military sites are linked by the H-1, H-2, and H-3 Interstates, which lead through long tunnels, over soaring viaducts, and past breathtaking landscapes, making them a blast to drive even for civilians.

Princess Kaʻiulani,
Hawaii's last princess
(1875-1899).
Photographed circa
1897.

Waikīkī rice fields, 1920

Sun, Sand, Surf . . . and Sophistication: Hawai'i Today

The natural beauty of the Hawaiian Islands contributes to a lifestyle that is one of the state's most important resources. Six to seven million tourists visit Hawai'i annually, many of them just for the sun, sand, and surf. Beautiful beaches are what come to mind first when one dreams of Hawai'i, and all the islands are ringed with spectacular ones. Even the perfect beach can still be found—that one with no footprints. Environmental scientist, Dr. Stephen P. Leatherman, a.k.a. Dr. Beach, consistently names Hawai'i's beaches the best in America.

With this sort of scenery and perfect weather year round, it's no wonder that outdoor sports have always been important in Hawai'i. Ancient chiefs used to reserve the best beaches for themselves, but now the commoners swarm to their favorite spots. Residents and tourists ride the waves of Waikīkī like the Hawaiians of long ago, watch the big wave surfers ride mountains of blue water at Waimea Bay, and windsurf at Kailua Beach on O'ahu and Ho'okipa Beach on Maui. Divers at Hanauma Bay, Molokini Island, and Hawai'i's many other diving meccas say there is no equal to Hawai'i's underwater dream world, and whale watchers come especially to the coast of Maui to sit for days watching these denizens of the deep frolic offshore. Golfers tee off over the blue Pacific at Mauna Kea's 3rd hole and take on "The Challenge at Mānele" Golf Course on Lāna'i. On Kaua'i, plant-lovers stroll through Allerton and Limahuli Botanical Gardens, and intrepid hikers trek along the narrow Kalalau mountain trail through tangled

Hula dancers

rainforests, totally unafraid of poisonous snakes and spiders or long-teethed beasts—Hawai'i has none at all.

While most of the world knows of the islands' natural treasures, fewer are aware of their many cultural ones. The Honolulu Academy of Arts holds extensive Western and Eastern collections, and a growing art scene flourishes in downtown Honolulu and in the galleries of Maui. The Polynesian Cultural Center showcases Pacific cultures and crafts. Ethnic restaurants offer local food with a Pacific Rim touch. The island music scene thrives, with melodies ranging from the deep throb of ancient hula to the soaring sweet notes of the Honolulu Symphony and lounge bars and outdoor stages offering mellow slack-key guitar, reggae, jazz, blues, rock, and hip-hop. If all this doesn't keep a family busy, there's always the movies—often one filmed right here in Hawai'i.

Despite drastic change and extensive development, the beauty of the Hawaiian Islands and the aloha spirit of the Hawaiian people still prevail. Everyone who comes to the Hawaiian Islands undergoes a sea change: formal businessmen from Connecticut and Canton, for example, can be found in flower-patterned aloha shirts every "Aloha Friday." The Hawaiian host culture is the cornerstone of Hawai'i's uniqueness, and today, growing cultural awareness and appreciation are beginning to preserve not just the fun trimmings, but also the language, traditions, and customs of the Hawaiians, as well as of the other cultures that call Hawai'i their home.

On his visit to the islands, Jack London was inspired to write, "By their language may ye know them and in what other land save this one is the commonest form of greeting, not 'Good day.' Nor 'How d'ye do,' but 'Love'? That greeting is Aloha—love, I love you, my love to you." The Aloha Spirit transcends the realities of the twentieth century. Unexpectedly, it pops up again and again in the smiling eyes and generosity of the Hawaiians, eager to share their beautiful islands with others. Hopefully, that spirit will always bless and preserve the beauty of the Hawaiian Islands and its peoples—maybe even spread around the world.

Children of plantation workers, 1920

Praise to Pele: The Volcanoes

Steam rises as red hot lava hits the ocean.

Hawai'i Volcanoes National Park

Enter not prayerless the house of Pele.
—Hawaiian Proverb

Kīlauea Volcano, the red-hot heart of Hawai'i Volcanoes National Park on the Big Island of Hawai'i, lives up to its name, which is Hawaiian for "spewing and much spreading." The most continuously active volcano on earth, Kīlauea is estimated to have first erupted 300,000 to 600,000 years ago and shows no sign of quitting any time soon. The present eruption at Kīlauea started in splendor in 1983. Over the last 20 years, lava from this eruption has buried more than 43 square miles of land and swallowed over 200 homes—but it has also added 510 acres to the Island of Hawai'i. The volcano's eruptions vary from jetting fountains 1,900 feet high to oozing streams. This is because lava itself takes many different forms: The common variety, named ʻaʻā by the Hawaiians, is a mixture of rough chunks of basalt that moves slowly but can cover extensive areas. *Pāhoehoe*, a liquid form of lava that pours out at temperatures of around 2,000 degrees, travels farther and faster than ʻaʻā and forms fields of fantastical shapes and designs. Lava also congeals into lava droplets, called Pele's tears, and green gem-like stones, called peridots or Pele's diamonds. Shimmering strands of volcanic glass are known as Pele's hair.

The flow of lava is unpredictable. Scientists at the Hawaiian Volcano Observatory monitor Kīlauea's activity constantly, mapping lava flows in an attempt to predict the direction a flow could take and the point at which it would become necessary to begin evacuations. Native Hawaiians place less faith in such things: "At this point, because of Pele's whim, the ocean entry is at this site," the park's spokeswoman says, adding that the unpredictability of the viewing makes it futile to plan ahead.

Previous page: Hawai'i Volcanoes National Park

The fire goddess Pele was worshipped by all in ancient Hawai'i and is still openly worshipped by some on the islands today. For more than a thousand years, she has been appeased by offerings of pigs, sacred red berries, and even a man or two. Throughout the park, offerings to the goddess still abound, though today they are mostly lava rocks wrapped in ti-leaves and flower leis. Many people say they have seen the goddess either as a beautiful young girl or an old woman. In whatever form she appears, it is best to proceed with caution whenever one encounters a fiery-eyed woman on the islands, and remember: taking lava rock from the volcano is said to bring down Pele's wrath. Each year, more than two thousand pounds of the rocks are returned to Hawai'i Volcanoes National Park from all over the world. Accompanying the rocks are usually letters of apology like this one:

Dear Volcano National Park,

Please return Pele's children to her with our gift . . . . In the last month, we have had an auto accident, our house was broken into and our plane crashed on landing in Dallas! We have heard enough strange but true stories about people who steal bits and pieces from parks and how Madame Pele does not appreciate being flung about by infidels. I am returning this lava as my family and I are moving to Hawaii . . . and I do not want to take any chances of irritating you know who. P.S. I can't believe I'm writing this.

There are also—what a relief—follow-up letters thanking the goddess for taking away the curse!

Lava formations along Chain of Craters Road. This road descends 3,700 feet in 20 miles and ends where a 2003 lava flow crossed the road.

Lava Tubes

A lava tube is formed when the surface of a lava flow cools and solidifies while the still-molten interior continues to flow through and drain away. Miles of such tubes snake their way through the underground of the Hawaiian Islands. In ancient times, lava tubes and caves were used as hospices or shelters for women and children in times of war. Many of them were also used as burial caves, and some still contain price-less Hawaiian artifacts and carvings.

Thurston Lava Tube, accessed from Chain of Craters Road in Hawai'i Volcanoes National Park on the Big Island of Hawai'i, is one of the islands' few easily explored lava tubes. From the road, a path winds through a magical rainforest to the cavernous hole that is a collapsed portion of the tunnel roof. Curious explorers duck under the fern curtain and enter a large, dark, cool tunnel. Small lights along the walls show pale, slightly spooky hanging roots, which are home to rare cave-dwelling arthropods: small, pale insects with tiny eyes that do not see and wings that cannot fly. Water drips down the walls and every-thing feels moist—a strange contrast to the sulfur vents and hot lava fields that surround the forest.

In Kula Kai Caverns in coastal Ka'ū, the volcano goddess Pele has decorated thirty-foot-high caverns and miles of chocolate-colored lava tubes with lacey crystals and delicate, pointed stalactites. Inside the tubes are Hawaiian gourds, placed hundreds of years ago to catch the precious fresh water that drips from the rock ceiling. Charred sticks remain from long ago as well, the remnants of small, flaring kukui nut torches used by Hawaiians to make their way along in the dark.

Walking through the silent, dark lava tubes is a strange, out-of-this-world experience. Crawling through narrow tunnels can be scary and claus-trophobic. Dr. Yoshiko Sinoto, Senior Anthropologist at the Bishop Museum, tells of an absolute worst-case scenario which he experi-enced while exploring unsurveyed caves and lava tubes in Kona with a team from the museum in 1954. As the smallest member of the team, he was invariably asked to lead the way. He was never very happy about this: the thought of being stuck underground in the pitch-black tubes during an earthquake was often on his mind. To his horror, one mile into a narrow tube in Kona, the ground began to shake. He fell to the floor and crouched at the side of the tube as rocks tumbled down around him. It seemed to him a very long few minutes before the shaking stopped.

Lava Tree State Park

Hoary 'ohi'a tree trunks encrusted with lava stand in the cracked earth of Lava Tree State Park in Puna on the Big Island of Hawai'i. The tree trunks were engulfed by the lava in 1790, when an eruption at Kīlauea Volcano discharged more than thirty-seven million cubic yards of fast-flowing Pāhoehoe lava that flooded the 'ohi'a forest. The moisture inside the trees cooled the lava, which then formed a hard shell. During the same eruption, tremors cracked the earth and huge fissures opened, showing how unstable the Big Island really is. Many of the tree trunks still stand; others lie on the ground like mossy tunnels leading nowhere. Giant monkeypod trees balance precariously over the cavernous cracks, their roots cascading into dark holes below.

Mark Twain, visiting in 1866, wrote of Puna in his inimitable fashion:

The last lava flow occurred here so long ago that there are none now living who witnessed it. In one place it enclosed and burned down a grove of cocoa-nut trees, and the holes in the lava where the trunks stood are still visible; their sides retain the impression of the bark; the trees fell upon the burning river, and becoming partly submerged, left in it the perfect counterpart of every knot and branch and leaf, and even nut, for curiosity seekers of a long distant day to gaze upon and wonder at.

There were doubtless plenty of (native) sentinels on guard hereabouts at that time, but they did not leave casts of their figures in the lava as the Roman sentinels at Herculaneum and Pompeii did. . . . However, they had their merits; the Romans exhibited the higher pluck, but the (natives) showed the sounder judgment.

Punalu'u Black Sand Beach

Foamy white waves ice the dark chocolate sand of Punalu'u Beach in Ka'ū on the Big Island of Hawai'i. The source of the sand was a flow of chunky *a'ā* lava that exploded into sand particles when it hit the ocean. The shining black sand is a limited commodity, as the supply ended when the lava stopped. Huge amounts of the sand and sand dunes were washed away in 1868 and 1969 when tsunamis swept into the bay. The tsunami waves and continuous earthquakes in 1868 destroyed the small village of Punalu'u.

The word *punalu'u* means "spring diving," and the area is so named for the activity that used to take place there. Along the beach, fresh-water

springs bubble up out of the sand on the ocean bed, and Hawaiians of long ago would dive down with gourds to collect the water, stopping them with a shell plug or their palms as they passed through the saltwater.

A charming plaque near the beach pictures a child sleeping with a turtle and tells the legend of Kauila, a turtle that could shape-shift into a girl. The people of Punalu'u loved Kauila, for she protected their children and gave them the area's pure spring water. Large green sea turtles, now an endangered species, still nest at the beach. Happily unaware of their endangered status, they swim up for face-to-face encounters with snorkelers, munch seaweed offered by children, and crawl out of the water to bask on the black sand.

Nearby, on the small beach of Kōloa, the tiny water-worn stones said by the Hawaiians to "give birth" can be found scattered about. Missionary Reverend William Ellis, who traveled around the Big Island in 1823, reported what locals told him of this phenomenon:

> The interest attaching to them is derived from the curious belief still held by many natives with whom I have conversed that they are of different sexes and begat offspring which increase in size and in turn begat others of their kind. The males are of a smooth surface without noticeable indentations or pits. The females have these little pits in which their young are developed and in due time separate from their mothers to begin independent existence.

This might sound rather weird to the post-Enlightenment Westerner, but it may very well

A sea turtle rests on Punalu'u's black sands.

be that what the natives perceive as "birthing stones" are nothing more than what scientists have named "conglomerate stones." Such stones are formed when *Pāhoehoe* lava flows over a pebble beach at low tide. The molten lava envelopes individual pebbles, but does not melt them because they are cool. In this way, the pebble gains another layer, which technically does "increase its size," while the lava, in a manner of speaking, becomes "pregnant" with the pebble. As the ocean erodes the lava flow, the newly formed water-worn stones (as they are called when they are in this two-layer state) are deposited on the beach. Further friction with the tide wears away the outer layer of the conglomerate stones until, eventually, the smaller, original pebble trapped inside is released—or "born."

Mauna Kea Volcano

Snow, said to be the cloak of Poliʻahu, the snow goddess, covers the volcanic cones on the slopes of the massive Mauna Kea (White Mountain) on the Big Island of Hawaiʻi. The mountain rises 31,796 feet from the ocean floor, with 13,796 of them above sea level. The snow goddess has kept the top of the mountain under her mantle of snow and ice despite the eruptions of molten rock and fire hurled by her rival, the volcano goddess Pele, from nearby Mauna Loa.

Mauna Kea has always been a sacred mountain to the Hawaiians. In ancient times it was said to be the gateway to heaven, and *Kāhuna*, or priests, climbed to this far and lofty summit to be closer to the gods. Today, the dormant volcano's height, remote location, and unpolluted atmosphere make it a superb place for astronomical observation and extreme science. Mushroom-domed observatories containing powerful telescopes crowd the summit, and in them nations from all over the world strain for a better view of what's out there. With the completion of the Keck Observatory, which holds the two largest optical telescopes in the world, the summit became the undisputed top vantage point on earth for peering into space. The University of Hawaiʻi is directly involved with NASA's space mission explorations, and on July 3, 2005, that cooperation paid off big when astronomers gathered at Mauna Kea to observe NASA's Deep Impact Space Probe connect with the nucleus of a comet that is as old as the solar system itself. The newest telescope within the Mauna Kea Science Reserve is Japan's Subaru, a $400 million supertelescope. According to the National Astronomical Observatory of Japan, the telescope "can now see almost all the way to the beginning of time itself."

Astronomers and students live in residences just below the mountain's summit, at about the 9,600-foot level. In the late afternoon, the residences are quiet: astronomers work at night. At such high altitudes the air is thin, and people need to become acclimatized to the lack of oxygen. Even then, those who work here need to descend to a lower elevation every four days. A student relates that at 14,000 feet human brains don't work that well and he has to think extra hard even with simple addition and subtraction calculations—a major concern for scientists trying to contemplate the origin of the universe! To top it all off, the weather on the mountain is freezing even in summer, and the winds are so

Mauna Kea observatories.

strong that they seem capable of easily lifting up any takers for a quick flight to the Kona beaches below.

Visitors are allowed to drive to Mauna Kea's summit during daylight hours. The terrain on the way up is extraterrestrial, and a four-wheel-drive vehicle is necessary to drive the narrow, steep road. From the high peak, the snow-tipped volcanic cones below look like inverted ice-cream cones. Permission is needed to visit the University of Hawai'i Observatory on the peak of Mauna Kea. Inside the observatory, a massive telescope peers into space and projects the images onto a screen. Miraculously, it seems, the thousands of little dots with a red tinge (an outer galaxy), though light years away in distance and time, can somehow be viewed from the top of the sacred Mauna Kea.

Haleakalā

Located on the island of Maui, Haleakalā, "House of the Sun," is the world's largest dormant volcano. Mists surround the 10,023-foot high summit, and clouds float far below. The volcano is the strongest natural power point in the United States, sitting like a mighty pyramid in the Pacific. Seismic activity there continues, and scientists predict that the mighty Haleakalā will one day erupt again. Haleakalā's crater, formed by erosion, is an awesome sight: a Mars-like playing field that could hold Manhattan, swirled by red, ochre, cream, beige, and chocolate, and dotted with peaked cinder cones up to 600 feet in height.

Haleakalā was a sacred mountain to the ancient Hawaiians, the place where the prankster god Maui lassoed the sun so that the islands would have more sunlight. (It really worked!) *Kāhuna* came here to pray, and rival *Kāhuna* groups fought for dominance of the site. In a way, their legacy is still carried on today by an abundance of star-gazers, also of rival factions—or at least philosophies. Atop Haleakalā, so many astronomical centers have sprung up that locals have nicknamed the area "Science City." Around the base of the volcano, however, congregate students of higher consciousness, attracted from around the world by the energy force here. According to park ranger and naturalist Mike Townsend, there might be something to this latter phenomenon: the huge, iron-rich cinder cone called Magnetic Peak has a magnetic field strong enough to deflect a compass needle. The closest town to Haleakalā, Makawao, is said to share this energy. As a result, it has an extraordinary wealth of healers, not to mention specialists, teachers, and guides in shamanic journeying; axiational, spiritual, and holistic healing; Chinese herbal medicine; craniosacral and horse-whispering therapy; iridology; psychic consulting; rebirthing; ascension acceleration; feng shui; and many more unusual adventures.

Indeed, there is energy on Haleakalā. Whether photographers looking for splendid sunrises, hikers headed for the crater floor, or intrepid cyclists who risk life and limb for the exhilarating, 38-mile zigzag ride to the bottom of the mountain, hundreds of visitors arrive here daily to bask in the majesty of the House of the Sun.

Kapo's Kingdom:
The Wildness and the Wet

Waipi'o Valley

Vibrantly green with sheer cliffs and shimmering waterfalls that plunge to a black sand beach, Waipi'o Valley on the Hāmākua Coast of the Big Island of Hawai'i is a hauntingly beautiful place. Hidden in the folds of its sharply serrated mountains are the dark secrets of the gods who lived there long, long ago, the gods whose stories are told in ancient chants and legends. According to these, the valley was the home of King Wakea, the legendary sky-father and ancestor of all Hawaiians. A young peasant boy called 'Umi, the offspring of a romantic encounter between another king and a beautiful commoner, came here to meet his royal father and to claim his heritage and became a mighty king himself.

Kū, the mighty god of war, was also honored in Waipi'o Valley. Tumbling stone walls and plat-

forms of dark lava rock mark the remains of six large *luakini heiau*, temples of war and human sacrifice, where vanquished enemies and breakers of the *kapu*, sacred law, were sacrificed to this hungry god. In 1873, just sixty-four years after the last human sacrifice lay on those altars, an intrepid woman explorer named Isabella Bird visited Waipi'o Valley. In her book *Six Months in the Sandwich Islands*, she wrote:

One of the legends told me concerning this lovely valley is that King 'Umi, having vanquished the kings of the six divisions of Hawai'i, was sacrificing captives in one of these heiaus, when the voice of his god, Kū-a-hilo, was heard from the clouds demanding more slaughter. Fresh human blood streamed from the altars, but the insatiable demon

Previous page: Lanaka Beach, O'ahu

continued to call for more, till 'Umi had sacrificed all the captives and all his own men but one, whom he at first refused to give up, as he was a great favorite, but Kū-a-hilo thundered from heaven, till the favorite warrior was slain, and only the king and the sacrificing priest remained.

Such a valley, surrounded by brooding cliffs pitted with secret burial caves, is sure to be walked by the "night marchers," spirits of chiefs and warriors of long ago marching in procession. Linda Beech, a doctor of psychology who has lived in Waipi'o Valley for 40 years, has heard the chanting and drums of these ghostly armies. At first, she thought the local Hawaiians were holding a ceremony at the nearby waterfall, so she went to listen to the music and to meet her neighbors. But the chanting always stopped just as she arrived at the falls. Linda believes that, after hundreds of years of human sacrifice in the valley, people and rituals are lost in time and our senses pick up on their resonance.

Today, only about 50 people live in isolated Waipi'o Valley, most of them taro farmers and fishermen. The lookout on the cliffs offers a magnificent view of the valley below, and a four-wheel-drive van called the Waipi'o Valley Shuttle carries visitors down the 2,300-foot cliff into the valley itself.

View from Waipi'o Lookout

'Ohe'o Gulch (Seven Sacred Pools)

Deep pools and cascading waterfalls give this site in Kīpahulu, East Maui its aura of *mana*, or power. The pools were given their more popular name, Seven Sacred Pools, by the owner of the Hotel Hāna Maui in 1947 to attract visitors—and it worked! However, there are actually many more than seven pools, and the correct name for the area is 'Ohe'o Gulch. Above the gulch, shimmering Waimoku Falls cascades 400 feet over a cliff into the fast-flowing 'Ohe'o Stream, which gushes onward to the coast through a series of large pools and tumbling waterfalls. Such inviting plunge-pools were once reserved for the pleasure of the *ali'i*, the chiefs, but today are wonderful places to swim even for commoners.

The hike to Waimoku Falls passes through Kīpahulu Bamboo Forest, a magical world of green darkness and slivers of sunlight filled with the clicking and creaking of towering bamboo. This is *'Ohe'o-o-Kapo*, the bamboo of Kapo, the goddess of healing, hula, and fierce sorcery. The bamboo represents her slender, swaying form, as she is commemorated in an ancient hula chant. Most stories of her tell of mischief, such as those of young men who follow a beautiful girl into the wildwood, fall into a trance and dream of sweet delight, only to awake and find themselves clutching a tree. Hikers on the Kīpahulu trail can build the necessary strength for such an encounter by sampling a smorgasbord of fruits: pink-fleshed guava, juicy mountain apples, sweet passion fruit, and even a sip of nectar from yellow ginger blossoms.

Iao Valley State Park

'Io dwelt within the breathing space of
*   immensity,*
The universe was in darkness with water
*   everywhere,*
There was no glimmer of dawn, no clearness,
*   no light,*
And he began by saying these words. . .
Darkness, become a light-possessing darkness!
And at once light appeared.

                                                    —Polynesian chant

'Iao Valley, also known as the "Valley of the Kings," is one of the most sacred and historically important sites on Maui. It is believed ancient Hawaiians named this vally 'Īao, (Supreme Light) in honor of 'Io, the supreme creator god. The valley is the eroded caldera of the extinct volcanoes now called the West Maui Mountains and the amphitheater where four streams meet. It was once a sacred place reserved for chiefs, who made pilgrimages here to experience the valley's *mana*, or power, and the mountains are still home to the secret burial caves of many high chiefs. 'Īao Valley State Park offers visitors a meandering path that leads past lush native plants, over a bridge, and up to a pavilion with views of the hushed, misty ravine. At the bottom of the valley, the bubbling stream has a series of refreshing pools. Much of this part of Maui is virtually impenetrable, but helicopter trips do offer breath-taking glimpses of untouched, secret waterfalls.

Ke'anae Peninsula

The serpentine road to Hāna in East Maui snakes by Ke'anae Peninsula, passing through a jungle of breadfruit, koa, kukui, mountain apple, paperbark, mango, guava, and hau trees. Wild ginger perfumes the air, and sparkling waterfalls refresh the toes. Here, on the lava peninsula that time forgot, the old village of Ke'anae stands dreaming. Life at Ke'anae is different: the spirit is authentically Hawaiian. Here, farmers grow taro in neat, square patches, children pick 'opihi (limpets) off the jagged black rocks, and fishermen head out to sea from an ancient canoe landing. The small Ke'anae Congregational Church, built in 1860 of lava rocks and coral mortar, is the community's tallest building: its spire is as tall as the swaying coconut palms. The tsunami of 1946 washed away nearly every building on the small peninsula, but the church was left standing. At the village's one tiny store, banana bread is sold still warm from the oven by the owner—who sports an even warmer smile.

Previous page: West Maui Mountains and town of Kahului

Mokoli'i Island (Chinaman's Hat)

Off the coast of Windward O'ahu is a small, cone-shaped island of the name Mokoli'i, but better known as "Chinaman's Hat." The island is a sea stack, part of the major Ko'olau Mountain Range formed by the Ko'olau Volcano, which once extended far out into the ocean. Pretty Mokoli'i is roughly 600 yards offshore, and islet seekers can float over on surfboards or wade over the reef at low tide. The far side of the island—the secret side—holds a tiny cove of golden sand sprinkled with cream and lavender cowry shells and washed by tide pools carved into the lava rock shelf.

The name Mokoli'i means "little mo'o," or dragon. A legend about the name tells the story of Hi'iaka, sister of Pele, the volcano goddess. She was traveling along the coast of Kāne'ohe Bay when she was confronted by a mo'o, a dragon lizard. The mo'o challenged her and wouldn't let her pass. Luckily, Hi'iaka was one of those powerful young goddesses who knew just how to handle dragons: She cut the monster in half and threw the tail into the ocean, where it became known as Mokoli'i Island.

Pu'u Pehe
(Sweetheart Rock)

The rock of Pu'u Pehe, or "Sweetheart Rock," as it is more popularly known, is an eighty-foot sea stack sculpted by waves in the deep blue waters of Pu'u Pehe Cove in Lāna'i's Mānele Bay. Legend says that Pu'u Pehe, a beautiful young girl from Maui, was captured by a young warrior from Lāna'i as "the joint prize of love and war." She was so beautiful that he feared losing her, and so he hid her in the sea cave of Malauea. One day he set out to fill their gourd with water, leaving his love to prepare their meal. As he returned, he saw a storm blowing into the coast. Frantically he raced the miles down the slope to rescue his bride, but by the time he arrived, the storm waves had already swept into the cave and drowned her. In grief, the young warrior retrieved her body and buried it at the top of the sea stack. He then leaped into the ocean below, taking his own life and joining his beloved.

An old chant sings his sorrow:

Where are you, O Pu'u Pehe?
Are you in the cave of Malauea?
Shall I bring you sweet water?
The water of the mountain?
Shall I bring the uwau bird?
The pala fern and the ohelo berry?

You are baking the honu
And the red, sweet hala,
Shall I pound the kalo of Maui?
Shall we dip in the gourd together?
The bird and the fish are bitter
And the mountain water is sour.
I shall drink it no more;
I shall drink it with 'Aipuhi,
The great shark of Mānele.

Moloka'i Sea Cliffs

The highest sea cliffs in the world tower 3,500 feet over the surging ocean on the wild northwest coast of Moloka'i. Resembling enormous fern-covered walls, the cliffs stretch from the wild surf to the clouds, split by deep chasms and streaming waterfalls. Not many people travel to the area's sea cliffs, remote valleys, sea caves, sea arches, and islets; local fishermen and adventurous kayakers are the only sailors of these waters. One such brave soul, author and explorer Audrey Sutherland, hiked, swam, and kayaked the remote coast eighteen times. In her book Paddling My Own Canoe, she describes the area:

> Ahead were the highest waterfalls of the coast. A dozen or more emerge from the plateau above, and because of heavy rainfall they were superb that year. Five of them are nearly three thousand feet high, but they do not make a simple, single drop. The cliff is not quite vertical; it leans back at a seventy-degree angle. Down the green slope the white water slides and splashes, bounces outward, touches and vaults again. Wailele, leaping water, catches the wind and sheets across the slope, then spirals upward with the air currents. The twisted sprays reflect the light in a thousand rainbows, drift sideward again, and become part of the next plumed cascade along the precipice.

For those not quite so courageous as Ms. Sutherland, a helicopter ride is always a good option.

Opposite: Rock formation on Pu'u Pehe shore

Left: The 45-foot
high Waimea
Falls is the focal
point of the park.

Waimea Falls Park

On nights of the full moon, Waimea Falls Park welcomes visitors to its moonlit paths. The spreading trees appear like a lacey canopy over the winding walkways, and the sweet smell of ginger fills the air. The 1,875-acre valley, managed by the Audubon Society, has a wonderful collection of over 6,000 species of rare plants and flowers as well as hundreds of magnificent trees. Deep in the park, Waimea Falls tumbles into a deep, reddish pool, believed by Hawaiians to have healing powers.

This lovely place was once a sacred valley, a dwelling place of powerful chiefs. A small temple to the god of agriculture, Lono, and numerous remains of ancient dwellings make this the most culturally significant site on the North Shore of O'ahu. A large sacrificial temple, Pu'uomahuka Heiau, looms over the park. In 1793, after the tragic death of Captain Cook, Vancouver's ship anchored in this idyllic bay and three English sailors went ashore to fetch water from the stream. Warriors watched from the hill above— ferocious warriors, loyal to Chief Kahekili, who claimed the god of thunder as his ancestor. Like Kahekili, half of their bodies were completely tattooed, including the insides of their eyelids. They noted the sailors' advanced European weapons and coveted what they saw. Storming down the hill, they captured and killed the sailors and burned their bodies on the stone altar of Pu'uomahuka Heiau. Today, a newly built wooden altar there holds fruit, flowers, and ti-leaf wrapped lava rocks, showing that the old gods have not been forgotten.

Kualoa Valley

Emerald green Kualoa Valley, nestled under the fluted columns and deep gorges of the Ko'olau Mountains, was once one of the most sacred places on the island of O'ahu. The cherished newborn children of chiefs lived in this *kapu* area (a sacred area forbidden to commoners) with their foster parents, and they learned here the sacred chants and how to fight

and rule. Fishermen in passing canoes lowered their sails in deference to the royal children.

Around 1775, Kahahana, a young chief, became ruler of the region. His uncle, the wily Maui chief Kahekili, asked for Kualoa Valley as a reward for having raised Kahahana. The young chief was agreeable to the request, but his *kahuna* warned:

> O chief! If you give away these things your authority will be lost, and you will cease to be a ruler. To Kualoa belong the watercourses of your ancestors [and] the sacred drums. Without the ivory that drifts ashore, you could not offer to the gods the first victim slain in battle; it would be for Kahekili to offer it on Maui, and the rule would become his. You would no longer be ruler . . . and be sure not to conceal from me any further secret message that Kahekili may send.

Unfortunately, not much later Kahekili poisoned Kahahana's mind against his faithful *kahuna*, and Kahahana treacherously murdered both the *kahuna* and his son. Kahekili, having removed his main opposition, then invaded O'ahu and routed Kahahana's warriors, and Kualoa became his.

The Ko'olau Mountains, holding the sacred burial cave of O'ahu's highest chiefs, are said to be full of such treasures as sacred sea ivory, carved idols, and feathered capes. Residents hear drums at night, and motor vehicle accidents are blamed on spooky sightings of ghostly night marchers who cross the road as they follow their ancient coastal highway. When building his new home, John Morgan, owner of beautiful Kualoa Ranch, was warned by his Hawaiian paniolo, cowboys, that he was building on the night marchers' path; that is, ghostly armies would be walking right past his house on a regular basis. He figured, why risk it? and relocated the house.

Kalalau Valley

Dreamlike Kalalau Valley in North Kauaʻi is the last of the incomparably beautiful valleys on the Kalalau Trail, a strenuous hike that begins at Kēʻē Beach and continues eleven miles along the Nā Pali Coast. Only at the end does one get to experience the splendor of the trail's namesake: mists wreathe green spires, sculptured ridges, and deep gorges; surf crashes onto a powdery strip of sand; and at the far end of the valley, a waterfall cascades into a deep pool. The valley's enchanting beauty can also be seen more easily by looking down from the Kalalau Valley Overlook, located on the high, mountainous rim of Kōkeʻe State Park.

In 1893, the isolated valley became the rocky lair of Koʻolau the Leper. Koʻolau was a cowboy who married his childhood sweetheart, Piʻilani, and they had a little son. Somehow, Koʻolau contracted the terrible disease, which was highly feared because it was contagious and incurable. Lepers in those days were forcibly taken to a leper settlement on the island of Molokaʻi, called by Hawaiians "the grave of living death." Many resisted going there, including Koʻolau: he vowed he would never be taken to Molokaʻi alive. He and Piʻilani and their young son fled to the remote Kalalau Valley, where they made their home in a cave and lived off the land. Piʻilani sometimes scaled the steep cliffs of the valley to fetch food for her family from the few Hawaiian families in the area.

Koʻolau wanted only to be left in peace, but authorities heard of his whereabouts and sent out a deputy and a large party of armed men to capture him. Koʻolau was an expert marksman, and he knew his pursuers well. Not wanting to fire on them, he warned that he, too, was armed, but the men were determined to bring him in. Resisting arrest, Koʻolau shot and killed the deputy and two of the armed men. After that, no one dared to hunt Koʻolau.

The family lived in the caves of Kalalau for four years. Then, tragically, the son contracted leprosy and died; shortly afterwards, Koʻolau also died. Alone, Piʻilani emerged from the valley in 1897. She thought she would be punished or even jailed, but was allowed to remain free. In a beautiful, dramatic poem telling of their life, Piʻilani wrote:

During the years of wandering in the wilderness of Kalalau, we climbed the steep ridges, then descended into the headlong depths of valleys, we trolled the mountainous regions and were watchful in the underbrush, we dwelt in the nooks and crannies, and this entire valley from its high cliffs to the flat terraces of earth became our home, and the dark clouds of Kāne were our ridgepole. . . . They [Koʻolau and their son] sleep in the bosom of Kalalau but will live again in living memories.

Waimea Canyon State Park

Slicing through West Kaua'i is the "Grand Canyon of the Pacific": the 3,500-foot-deep gorge called Waimea Canyon, a wilderness of deep canyons and gorges of volcanic rock carved over thousands of years by the streams that flood from Mount Wai'ale'ale and the Alaka'i Swamp. A steep road winds up to Waimea Canyon State Park, and every lookout along the way gives a spectacular view of the mountain fortress, its walls painted ochre, mauve, and red by shadow. Trails lead around the ridge on top of the canyon, into gorges, through native forests, and on to Kōke'e State Park and the panorama of the coast.

The Kukui Trail, a series of switchbacks, starts as a pretty nature trail and leads two and a half miles down to Waimea River at the bottom of the canyon. The river is fed from above by the vast wetlands of the high Alaka'i Swamp, and the abundance of swamp vegetation gives it a tea-like color. Native trees grow along the sides of the canyon: wiliwili, with claw-shaped flowers, and pale-leafed kukui trees, with the dark, oil-rich kukui nuts that Hawaiians used for candles. Streams from the high mountaintop drop down the canyon walls, creating thin, silver waterfalls.

Terraces and remains of stone platforms in the canyon are evidence that the area was inhabited long ago. Some say it is still walked by night marchers, ghostly processions of warriors and chiefs. As evening falls, nervous hikers remember that darkness comes early down in the canyons, and it's a long, hard hike back to the top.

Thrilling helicopter flights show the canyon from a different perspective. Sweeping down side canyons in a real-life video game, they fall along with the steep walls that drop sheer for half a mile to the canyon floor, then burst out into the blue of the open sky and circle one of the magnificent amphitheater valleys streaked by waterfalls.

Wailua River Valley

This is the moment
Of sweet Aloha.
I will love you longer than forever
Promise me that you will leave me never...
Now that we are one
Clouds won't hide the sun
Blue skies of Hawai'i smile
On this, our wedding day.
      —"Hawaiian Wedding Song,"
            by Charles E. King

Tour boats and kayaks cruise down the winding Wailua River in East Kaua'i, lured by the green beauty of the huge lava cave called Fern Grotto. Even bridal couples come to say their vows in nature's magical cathedral of misty hanging ferns, accompanied by musicians playing the "Hawaiian Wedding Song."

Wailua means "sacred or ghostly water," and the Wailua River meanders through a valley that was once considered sacred from the heights of its mountains all the way to where it meets the sea. Every morning, the first rays of the sun to touch the mouth of the Wailua River do so at the stone remains of Hikina'akalā Heiau, "Temple of the Rising Sun." Centuries ago, priests gathered here at dawn to welcome the day with chanting and singing and dance a hula to tilted wooden idols that swayed in the surf.

Further up the mountain on the King's Highway, ancient stone ruins tell of life and death long ago. Holoholukū Heiau, a feared temple of human sacrifice, still broods there. The large boulders and slab adjacent to the temple were once used as birthing stones, a place where many royal babies were born. A chant tells of the importance of giving birth at these stones:

> *The child of a chief born at Holoholukū becomes a high chief.*
> *The child of a commoner born at Holoholukū becomes a chief also.*
> *The child of a high chief born outside of Holoholukū is no chief, a commoner he!*

At the top of the ridge, Poli'ahu Heiau, a large war temple, occupies a commanding position

overlooking a vista of rainforest and the lovely 'Ōpaeka'a Falls.

This valley was once the home and religious seat of powerful kings and chiefs, fine-looking, strong men who were fond of surf riding. Whenever chiefs arrived by canoe at the mouth of the Wailua River, warriors would lift the canoes onto their shoulders and carry the esteemed descendants of the gods through the surf and up to the houses and *heiau*. Bell stones and drums announced the arrival of the chiefs, alerting commoners to stay out of the way. Wise ones did so, for a commoner whose shadow fell onto a high chief or any of his possessions was to be punished by death.

Kaua'i chiefs had the bluest blood in the islands and were highly desirable marriage partners. Kaumuali'i, a handsome chief from Wailua who became king of Kaua'i, possessed the highest lineage of any chief in all the islands. He had a powerful rival, though: the warlike Kamehameha the Great, who had already conquered the other islands and longed to conquer Kaua'i. Living under the constant threat of attack, King Kaumuali'i formed a short alliance with Russia to try to protect his kingdom. An ambitious Russian diplomat built three forts on Kaua'i, but was ordered to leave by Kamehameha. Even though Kamehameha did not technically control the island, the diplomat did not dare disobey him.

When Kamehameha died, he left a powerful widow, Queen Ka'ahumanu. The queen had a better plan for conquering Kaua'i: She sent her stepson and heir to the throne, Liholiho, to visit King Kaumuali'i and to invite him on board his boat. Liholiho then sailed back home to O'ahu, kidnapping the handsome king. Once in O'ahu, Kaumuali'i had another surprise: the six-foot-tall, three-hundred-pound Queen Ka'ahamanu. Despite the protests of the missionaries on the island, she married both the handsome Kaumuali'i and his handsome son, thereby conquering Kaua'i—something her great husband, Kamehameha, had never been able to do.

Fierce Chiefs and Feather
Gods: Remnants of the
Ancients

Pu'ukoholā Heiau

Fear falls upon me on the mountaintop
Fear of the passing night
Fear of the night approaching
Fear of the pregnant night
Fear of the breach of the law
Dread of the place of offering and the narrow
　　trail
Dread of the food and the waste part
　　remaining
Dread of the receding night
Awe of the night approaching.

　　　　　　—From the Kumulipo,
　　　　the Hawaiian creation chant

"Honor the supreme war god Kūka'ilimoku," a prophet told Kamehameha. "Build a mighty *luakini heiau* at Pu'ukoholā, and you will gain the whole kingdom without a scratch to your skin." In 1790, Kamehameha the Great built that mighty temple in a cove on a hill overlooking the ocean in South Kohala on the Big Island of Hawai'i. Workers formed a human chain twenty miles long to move rocks across the island from Pololū to Pu'ukoholā, where they used them to construct the massive stone temple's immense solid platforms and 20-foot-high lava walls.

Previous page: Pu'uhonua O Honaunau National Historical Park (Place of Refuge)

Kamehameha invited his cousin and enemy, Keōua, to the opening ceremony. Keōua was suspicious of the invitation, but didn't dare refuse it. As his army traveled through coastal Ka'ū on their way to the ceremony, Pele, the goddess of the volcano, rained molten lava upon them. Hundreds of the warriors were killed as they fled, their footprints becoming forever imprinted in the lava fields. Kamehameha took the event as proof of divine favor: Pele was on his side! Whether by accident or design, Keōua was speared on arrival at the cove and became the first offering on the great temple's stone altar. As prophesied, from that day on the war god Kūka'ilimoku backed Kamehameha.

The story of Kamehameha the Great, the ruler who united the Hawaiian Islands, is a fascinating saga strongly reminiscent of King Arthur and Excalibur: For years, priests prophesied the birth of a child who would conquer and rule all the islands, a mighty king—a killer of kings. This prophecy greatly disturbed Alapa'i, the ruling chief of the island of Hawai'i. He became even more disturbed when his young niece, the pregnant high chiefess Keku'iapoiwa, made public her desire to eat the eyeball of a shark. This was a fearful omen. Alapa'i was already suspicious about the paternity of the baby: Keku'iapoiwa had left her young husband on Hawai'i and spent many months visiting her royal family on Maui, and she was pregnant when she returned. The ruling chief of Maui, the mighty tattooed Kahekili, was Alapa'i's sworn enemy. Was Kahekili the father of Keku'iapoiwa's unborn child? Some taunting chants were making the rounds, claiming that Kahekili had sent a present to Alapa'i—and that he sent it with Keku'iapoiwa. Keku'iapoiwa's husband appears to have accepted the situation, but Alapa'i was seething.

Frightened, Keku'iapoiwa and her husband fled to the isolated plains of northern Hawai'i. As Halley's comet streaked through the sky, the baby was born. The newborn infant was immediately handed to a trusted warrior, who ran the long distance to the remote Waipi'o Valley and gave the baby to his wife to nurse along with her own newborn daughter. Alapa'i ordered his warriors to hunt and kill the baby; on Maui, Kahekili's family, who wanted no potential rivals, gave similar orders. Warriors came to the cave where the baby was hidden, but little Kamehameha lay snug and quiet, covered by tapa cloths. The child spent five years hidden in the isolated valley of Waipi'o—hence the name Kamehameha, "the lonely one."

Kamehameha became a fearsome warrior, but it took him many years of battle before he fulfilled his destiny of conquering the warlike chiefs and uniting the islands under his rule. In peace, he was a fair monarch who brought peace and prosperity to the kingdom of Hawai'i. He is still recognized as a great military strategist; and his statue stands in the Statuary Hall in the Capitol Building in Washington D.C.

Bishop Museum Hawai'i and Pacific Collections

The Bishop Museum, a fortress-like Victorian building in Honolulu on the island of O'ahu, is the repository of the greatest collection of Hawaiian and Pacific artifacts in the world. It holds the treasures of Princess Ruth, Queen Emma, and Princess Bernice Pauahi, whose husband, American Charles Bishop, combined the collections to start the Bishop Museum in 1889.

Who were the ancient Hawaiians? What did they and their world look like? The Bishop Museum holds the answers to these questions. The Hawaiian Hall, somber and glowing with the rich tones of koa wood, has priceless collections of ancestral relics and religious carvings, including carved idols. Among these is Kamehameha's war-god KūKā'ilimoku, a huge, leering sculpture that is the tallest Hawaiian sculpture ever found. And safe behind glass—but still looking wicked and untamed—is the red-feathered idol of Kū that Kamehameha carried into battle. The idol is approximately thirty inches tall and has glaring pearl-shell eyes, black-feathered eyebrows, and a snarling mouth with ninety-four dogteeth. The feathers on Kū's head

One of the Bishop Museum's many attractive exhibit halls.

were said to bristle as he was carried into battle, and his wild screams could be heard above the sounds of the fighting.

In front of the huge Kū statue stands a small model of Wahaʻula Heiau, "Red Mouth Temple." The model was built in the 1930s with lava stones from the original *heiau*, the first terrible Hawaiian *luakini heiau*, temple of human sacrifice, built to honor Kū. After the exhibit's placement in the museum, a young repairman working on the museum's roof plunged through a skylight and fell to his death—right atop the *heiau* exhibit. Hawaiians said the heiau of Kū had claimed another human sacrifice.

Other regalia of the *aliʻi* in the Hawaiian Hall include priceless red- and yellow-feather capes, still as smooth and rich as velvet. One such cloak, thought to have belonged to Kamehameha I, required some 450,000 yellow feathers plucked from about 80,000 black honeycreepers, little birds with small tufts of bright yellow feathers that grow above and below their tails. The seven-foot-tall Kamehameha the Great also wore a crescent helmet similar to those worn by Roman soldiers. Feather helmets were not merely decorative: just beneath the downy-soft exterior was a dense structure of roots, which provided protection against the weapons of long ago.

The tiger-shark teeth on spears and clubs still glisten. Some koa wood calabashes and spittoons are even festooned with human teeth—a Home-and-Gardens sort of way of humiliating one's enemies. Gourd masks with dark, empty eyeholes are frightening reminders of the powerful *kāhuna*, priests. Water jugs formed from large, decorated gourds and storage baskets made from the aerial roots of vines tell of daily living and careful craftsmanship. Turtle shell bracelets, bone combs, and ornaments from whale ivory can still arouse envy in lady visitors today. Fascinating old sketches show the regal faces of long-ago *aliʻi*, royalty, and paintings by an artist from the first British sailing ships portray the arrival of Captain Cook.

In addition to these ancient Hawaiian artifacts, the Bishop Museum also contains a wealth of other interesting items. They include more than six million zoology specimens, from insects to birds and mammals; nearly half a million botany specimens; thousands of books, photographs, and maps; and a plethora of all sorts of cultural objects—to name just a few.

Above left: Feathered image of a deity said to be KūKāʻilimoku, "Kū the Snatcher of Land," ancestral war god of Kamehameha the Great.

Above right: Lifesize replica of a moai, *stone idol, from the Polynesian island of Rapa Nui.*

Pu'uhonua O Hōnaunau National Historical Park
(Place of Refuge)

In South Kona on the Big Island of Hawai'i, this tranquil-looking cove encircled by thick, ten-foot-high lava walls is now known as Pu'uhonua O Hōnaunau National Historical Park. However, as its name reveals, it was once a place of refuge, a sanctuary for vanquished warriors or breakers of the *kapu* law. In ancient Hawai'i, the *kapu*, sacred law, governed people's lives. The number of laws was daunting, and the penalty for transgression was always death. But here, oh! Here was a palm-shaded haven of thatched huts protected by large, ferocious idols and blessed by a temple containing sacred, royal bones. Once

inside these walls, a fugitive could shout the Hawaiian equivalent of *Home Free!* And after the temple priests performed cleansing rituals over the *kapu* breaker, he was considered by all—even his enemies—to be under the protection of the priests and the gods, and so could leave even the refuge in safety.

Even Queen Ka'ahumanu, the favorite wife of Kamehameha I, sought sanctuary here. The jealous king took many wives himself, but he declared the body of favorite but fickle Queen Ka'ahumanu *kapu* and forbidden in an effort to control her. This declaration of *kapu* meant that

Hale o Keawe Temple. Ki'i (wooden images) stand watch over this reconstruction of a temple and mausoleum.

Hawaiian tiki wood carvings of Ki'i, guardians of the place of refuge.

her lovers faced death if discovered, and some paid this extreme price. This did not always deter the young queen, though. In one instance, after offending the king she swam across the bay to the place of refuge, where she hid behind the stone now called Ka'ahumanu's Stone. Her small dog barked and betrayed her hiding place to Kamehameha. As usual, the long-suffering king forgave his favorite wife.

Explorer Isabella Bird, visiting Hawai'i in 1873, wrote, "Could any tradition of the Mosaic ordinance on this subject have traveled hither?" She notes that Joshua, following a directive given by God through Moses, named six cities in the Promised Land as places of refuge. Mark Twain, when traveling in Hawai'i in 1866, described the Place of Refuge in his usual inimitable fashion:

> In those days, if a man killed another anywhere on the island the relatives were privileged to take the murderer's life; and then a chase for life and liberty began—the outlawed criminal flying through pathless forests and over mountains and plain, with his hopes fixed upon the protecting walls of the City of Refuge, and the avenger of blood following hotly after him! Sometimes the race was kept up to the very gates of the temple, and the panting pair sped through long files of excited natives, who watched the contest with flashing eye and dilated nostril, encouraging the hunted refugee with sharp, inspiring ejaculations, and sending up a ringing shout of exultation when the saving gates closed upon him and the cheated pursuer sunk exhausted at the threshold. But sometimes the flying criminal fell under the hand of the avenger at the very door, when one more brave stride, one more brief second of time would have

brought his feet upon the sacred ground and barred him against all harm. Where did these isolated pagans get this idea of a City of Refuge—this ancient Oriental custom?

> This old sanctuary was sacred to all—even to rebels in arms and invading armies. Once within its walls, and confession made to the priest and absolution obtained, the wretch with a price upon his head could go forth without fear and without danger—he was tabu, and to harm him was death!

In 1819, Liholiho, Kamehameha II, abolished the *kapu* system, and the Place of Refuge was destroyed. However, the 1,000-foot-long Great Wall and the foundation of the temple, which held the bones of illustrious chiefs, were left intact. Later, these and the giant 'ohi'a wood statues of temple gods were reconstructed from sketches made by early European explorers. The thatched huts of the village were also rebuilt, and today visitors can sit under the palm trees and play checkers on ancient *konane* stone slabs or watch canoe builders carve with stone adzes. An ancient footpath winds along the coast and past a long, stone *holua* slide, on which chiefs once raced downhill on wooden sleds—the tropical equivalent of snowboarding.

Puakō Petroglyphs

Strange petroglyphs, like letters from the past, cover smooth squares of lava in the petroglyph fields of Puakō in South Kohala on the Big Island of Hawai'i. Over three thousand glyph units, considered some of the finest and oldest in Hawai'i, were carved here between 1000 and 1800 A.D. Other carvings of horses and cattle were added after Westerners arrived.

It is not known whether the petroglyphs were prayers to gods, accounts of notable events, or just doodles made to pass the time, but historians assume that the carvings did have some magic or religious function. Perhaps some petroglyphs were records of travelers who crossed these vast, lonely fields of lava: some show running men, and there is a long line of twenty-nine stick figures marching. In one touching petroglyph depicting the birth of a royal baby, the father holds the child's feet and carved rays streak from the child's head.

Hundreds of small holes and circles in the lava rocks, *Pōhaku piko*, once held the umbilical cords of babies. Carvings of a dog or a *mo'o*, dragon lizard, represent a supernatural spirit guarding the cord in the piko hole. Umbilical cords had to be very well hidden in ancient Hawai'i, for if rats found and ate the cord, it was considered a terrible omen: the child would grow up to be a thief and a disgrace to his family. Parents would sometimes give away babies whose umbilical cords disappeared from the holes, and "Pau piko ka'iole," "Umbilical cord gone to the rats," was a nasty insult no Hawaiian wanted to hear.

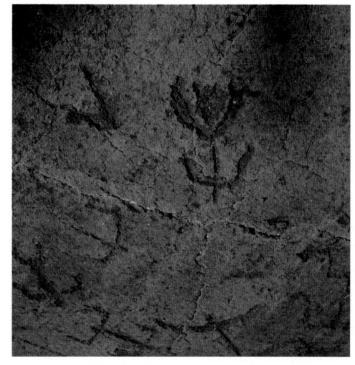

Ahu'ena Heiau

The leering idols of Ahu'ena Heiau, "Burning Altar," stand guard over the waters of Kailua Bay in Kona on the Big Island of Hawai'i. Before visitors even arrive at the temple, they can't help but notice Kōleamoku, the tallest of all the idols there. The god Kōleamoku's priests were experts in navigation, and he is crowned with the *kōlea*, golden plover, the bird said to have guided the Polynesians to Hawai'i. The restored temple, with thatched houses and an oracle tower, was rebuilt according to an 1816 sketch of the original temple by visiting French artist Choris.

This *heiau* was the final home of Kamehameha I. Age mellowed the warrior king, and he had the temple, originally a war temple of human sacrifice dedicated to Kū, rededicated to Lono, the god of agriculture. Kamehameha honored Lono by building the Hale O Lono, House of Lono, where he wisely held the captured gods of his enemies. He also built other houses to shelter all of the sorcery gods that he secured. When the great king was dying, his priests suggested a human sacrifice be offered in exchange for his life, but he refused. Just before he died, he whispered, "Enjoy quietly what I have made right." Kamehameha's bones were hidden and have never been found.

Seven days after the death of the mighty king, the ranking chiefs were summoned to Ahu'ena Heiau. Their gathering there marked the beginning of the end for the ancient Hawaiian sacred law and *kapu* system, which Kamehameha I had strongly upheld. With the support of two of Kamehameha's wives, the fearfully powerful Queen Keōpūolani and the fearlessly driven Queen Ka'ahumanu, Kamehameha's heir, Liholiho, ordered the temples and the images of the gods destroyed. In this historically unprecedented sequence of events, the Hawaiian people actually brought down their own gods.

Phallic Rock

Moloka'i mo' bettah.
 —Hawaiian saying in Pidgin English
 ("Moloka'i more better.")

Ka-ule-o-Nānāhoa, the "Penis of Nānāhoa," stands erect in a grove of ironwood trees in Pālā'au State Park on the island of Moloka'i. Nānāhoa, whose spirit is in this ancient fertility rock, is said to have been an impressive man who never, ever had a headache. But he made one crucial mistake: he got caught by his wife as he watched a young girl bathing. N⁻an⁻ahoa and his wife fought so furiously and for so long that the exasperated gods finally just turned them both into stone.

The six-foot-high natural stone said to be Nānāhoa is a legendary fertility tool with a reputation for making women visitors pregnant, both long ago and today. The historian Coelho tells of a time when the people had no children because husbands and wives were fighting. A *kahuna*, priest, advised the women to take offerings and sleep at the stone; when they returned home, all the women were pregnant. Women still come here to pray for a child, and there are many modern success stories. One recent validated report came from a woman who'd previously had her tubes tied—of course, such a stone can be a menace as well as a blessing!

Phallic rocks were thought to work by passing on male energy in the form of fertility to the people as well as the land and animals. For this reason, they are often found at ancient Hawaiian temples, and numerous small, oval, engraved stones were found at the site of this phallic rock. Such stones, some of which are now in the Bishop Museum, were placed at the phallic rock to be impregnated with its *mana*, powerful energy, then were taken home to promote crop and animal fertility.

As Moloka'i is also known as the Island of Powerful Prayer, wise visitors approach this rock cautiously.

Pi'ilanihale Heiau

Pi'ilanihale Heiau, the largest *heiau* on the Hawaiian Islands and a National Historic Landmark, stands on the wildly beautiful coast of Hāna in eastern Maui. Covering nearly three acres, the temple is twice as long as a football field, and every inch of the construction is unique. The thick, 50-foot-high stone walls are constructed of finely fitted lava rock without mortar of any kind. The immense north wall is composed of five curving, terraced platforms. A steep path leads up to the high altar platform, which overlooks two separate platforms connected by a central terrace with a mysterious, 40-foot-deep, stone-filled gully. Scattered throughout the rest of the temple are 23 pits and numerous upright sacred stones, possibly phallic rocks or fish gods.

Pi'ilanihale Heiau dates back to the fourteenth century, when it was the heart of a powerful ancient kingdom and the home of the royal Pi'ilani family of Maui. Yet, despite both its status and stature, the history of the *heiau* is shrouded in mystery and not referred to in any of the Hawaiian chants, those sole preservers of the islands' oral history. How is this possible? Chipper Wichman, director of the adjacent Kahanu Gardens, says that talking about the *heiau* might have been made *kapu*, forbidden by sacred law, because of a terrible family conflict.

Indeed, legends say that Chief Pi'ilani's two sons quarreled violently after his death. There were many reasons, but the main one was Kōleamoku, a beautiful girl surfer. Kōleamoku was betrothed to Lono-a-Pi'ilani, the eldest son of the deceased chief. However, while surfing one day, she met Kiha-a-Pi'ilani, the younger son, and they fell in love and married. After this, strained relations between the brothers were sprung, and Lono sought to kill Kiha. Kiha fled and joined forces with mighty 'Umi, king of Hawai'i, and together they vanquished Lono.

According to this same oral tradition, Kiha put a *kapu* on any talk of his brother, as well as on the boys' childhood home, the massive Pi'ilanihale Heiau. The great temple stood silent for centuries as vines smothered its lava walls. Hawaiian descendants of the family say they were forbidden as children to go near the *heiau*. Recently, however, the family received a grant to restore the temple, and the work was painstakingly but beautifully done. The mighty temple, still deeply respected and even somewhat *kapu*, can be seen from the surrounding Kahanu Gardens.

Nuʻuanu Pali Lookout

Where the steep pinnacles and jagged green peaks of the Nuʻuanu Pali cliffs tower over Windward Oʻahu, Nuʻuanu Pali Lookout offers a panoramic view of the lush valley, the blue ocean, and the small offshore islands below. The winds that funnel up from the valley are often so strong that giggling tourists are forced to hold on to their clothing and even to cling to each other.

There is a solemn quality to this mountain fortress, arising out of its somber history. In 1795, the fierce kings of Oʻahu and Hawaiʻi were on the warpath again. The ambitious Kamehameha I's plan to unite the islands was well underway: he had conquered Maui and Molokaʻi in quick succession, and now his great fleet of war canoes headed for Oʻahu. But Kalanikūpule, king of Oʻahu, was also an ambitious man, and he had an advantage: he had acquired Western cannons from a trading ship. Anticipating Kamehameha's attack, he positioned his cannons in notches hewn out of the high Pali ridges.

As Kamehameha's forces marched up the valley, Kalanikūpule's cannons and artillery bore down on and nearly defeated them. But Kamehameha is recognized as a great military strategist even today—and for good reason. To stop the slaughter inflicted by the cannons, he divided his troops, sending his fastest and strongest warriors to approach the Pali from two different ridge trails, thereby delivering a surprise attack from the rear. The forces converged on the cannons and quickly captured them.

The rest of Kamehameha's army now ascended from the valley. The Oʻahu army retreated, but was trapped on the high cliffs. More than a thousand of the desperate warriors leaped or were forced into the abyss below. During construction of Old Pali Road, workers found at the foot of the cliffs an estimated 800 skulls and other human bones, the remains of the defeated warriors. The Nuʻuanu Pali area is one of Hawaiʻi's most haunted places today. Night marchers, ghostly armies of warriors, are said to walk its trails on dark, misty nights when the wild wind wails.

'Alekoko Menehune Fish Pond

'Alekoko ("Rippling Blood") Menehune Fishpond, located near Lihu'e in Kaua'i, is said to be the handiwork of the legendary little people called the Menehune, who constructed it for a lazy chief called Pi. The small but strong Menehune had a reputation for hard, patient work—so much that legend says that their blood rippled in the water as they built this fishpond. Working only at night, Menehune passed boulders hand-to-hand along a double line that extended for 25 miles. Their method of rockwork, in which they chiseled each rock individually to fit them perfectly together, required immense labor and so was unique to these very early settlers of the islands. When the little people discovered that they were being spied on by Chief Pi, they left their worksite in anger, leaving holes in the fishpond's stone walls. To placate the angry workers, Chief Pi fed them their favorite food, red shrimp, and they finished the fishpond.

But were there really Menehune at all? Some researchers think that the word menehune derives from the word *manahune*, a Tahitian term of derision that means "commoner." An old Tahitian mele addressing manahune begins: "Go up to the mountains where you belong, far, far away up there . . . thou slaves of the ali'i (chiefs)." If indeed the Menehune were the manahune of Tahiti, it appears they took the hint, for they left the islands, leaving only traces of their stonework in remote valleys and on the far island of Nīhoa. On the other hand, in the early nineteenth century, 65 Menehune were listed in a population census of Kaua'i's isolated northern valleys. Most tales of the Menehune are set in Kaua'i, but all the islands claim sightings of these little people.

Ka-ulu-o-Laka Heiau, Temple of Hula

Enchanting Kēʻē Beach, nestled at the base of the fluted Pali on the north shore of Kauaʻi, was once the home of Laka, the goddess of hula. Fragmented terraces and a grassy platform are all that remain of a temple to the goddess, the Ka-ulu-o-Laka Heiau, where hula dancers were trained. The training was strict and subject to many sacred laws: during the entire training period, dancers could not cut their hair or nails, and certain foods and sexual intercourse were forbidden. They had to take great care when memorizing the chants—particularly the long genealogy chants of the royal families—because the spoken word contained powerful *mana*. A mistaken word or syllable could change the meaning of the chant and offend the temperamental gods or the chiefs, who would then kill the dancer.

In addition to great entertainment, the erotic hula was a form of worship. The purpose of some of the dances, for example, was to arouse the gods and thus bring about fertility in nature. Perhaps contrary to modern expectations, fertility was the province of men in ancient Hawaiʻi: men performed the fertility dances at the temple, and the reproductive powers of the chiefs were celebrated. Many chiefs even had their own *mele mai*, "genital chant"; King Kalākaua, for instance, had a chant that credited him with *hālala*—that is, being very well-endowed.

Kona village luaus

The naked breasts and seductive movements of hula dancers horrified early missionaries, who saw the hula as a pagan ritual. Under their influence, Queen Kaʻahumanu banned the hula in 1830, but it was revived in 1874 by King Kalākaua, who called it "the language of the heart and the heartbeat of the Hawaiian people." Mark Twain visited Hawaiʻi shortly after the hula's revival and wrote thereof:

> At night they feasted and the girls danced the lascivious hula-hula—a dance that is said to exhibit the very perfection of educated motion of limb and arm, hand, head and body, and the exactest uniformity of movement and accuracy of 'time.' It was performed by a circle of girls with no raiment on them to speak of, who went through an infinite variety of motions and figures without prompting, and yet so true was their 'time,' and in such perfect concert did they move that when they were placed in a straight line, hands, arms, bodies, limbs, and heads waved, swayed, gesticulated, bowed and undulated as if they were part and parcel of a single individual; and it was difficult to believe they were not moved in a body of some exquisite piece of mechanism.

Today, hula festivals are held in recognition of the importance of this traditional dance. The ancient sacred hula, which often sings praise to Pele, is particularly moving and powerful. Recognizing the beauty of the dance, Christian hula *hālau* groups dance the hula too, swaying gracefully and moving their outstretched arms and hands expressively as they give glory to God.

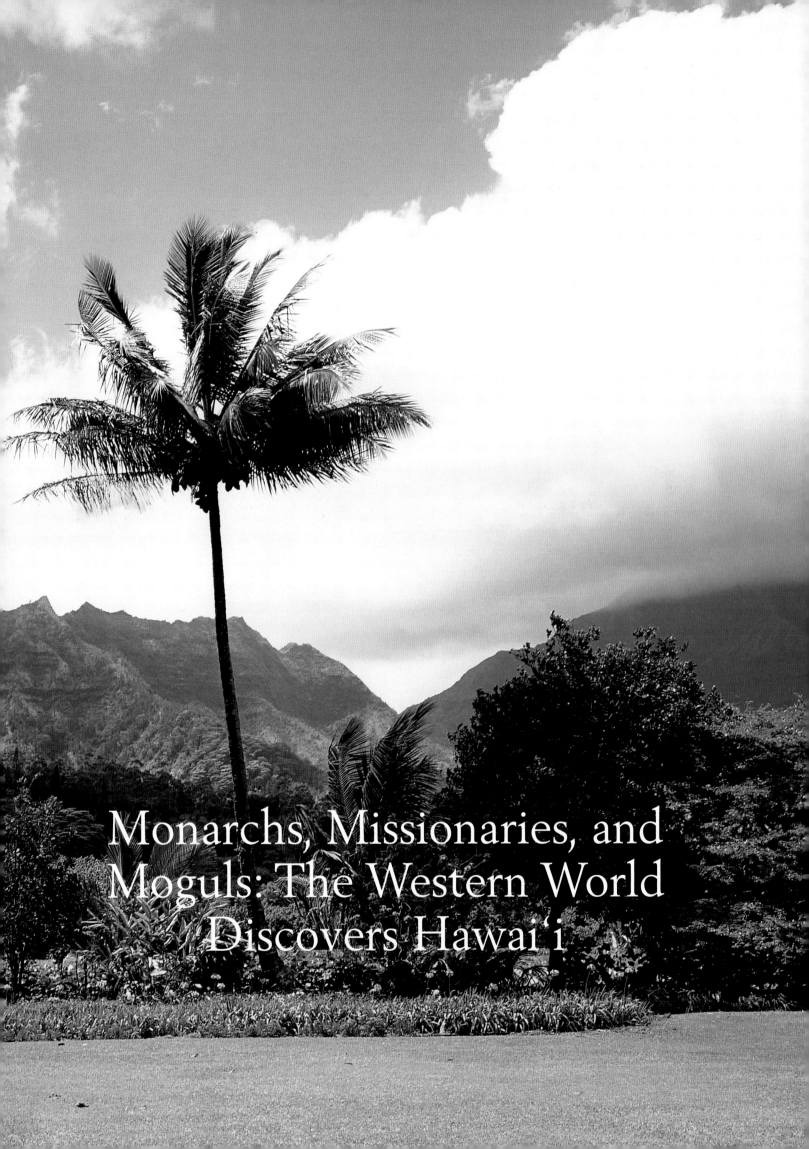

Monarchs, Missionaries, and Moguls: The Western World Discovers Hawai'i

Kealakekua Bay

Out in the crystal waters of Kealakekua (Path of the Gods) Bay off the Big Island of Hawai'i, a white marble obelisk commemorates Captain James Cook. In 1779, the Hawaiians here witnessed an astonishing sight: two British ships, HMS *Resolution* and *Discovery*, sailed into the cove. Their tall white sails resembled the *kapa* cloth standards carried by the priests of Lono, the god of farming and fertility. It had been prophesied that Lono would return to the islands one day during the harvest festival, and at the time of the ships' arrival, the Hawaiians were celebrating the harvest season. Everything seemed to fit together. Awestruck, a *kahuna* proclaimed the two "floating islands" of the English to be the temples of the great god Lono.

As the story is told by the official chronicler of the third voyage of Captain Cook, the crowds of natives that gathered on—and in—the water were innumerable. Captain Cook was thought to be the incarnation of Lono himself. Crowds prostrated themselves before him, and he was taken to nearby Hikiau Heiau, where he was plied with food and honored for hours with long, solemn chants and prayers.

During the weeks in which the ships were anchored in the bay, the British seamen were also treated as gods, and food and gifts were heaped upon them. A seaman reported: "We live now in the greatest Luxury, and as to the Choice and number of fine women there is hardly one among us that may not vie with the grand Turk himself." Aware that his crew carried syphilis, Captain Cook tried to keep the sailors from the willing Hawaiian women—a futile task.

Cook left the islands with generous supplies

Previous page: View of Hanalei Valley from Wai'oli Mission House

of pigs, fruit, and vegetables. Unfortunately, a storm at sea forced the ships to return. This puzzled the Hawaiians: it was not expected that Lono would return after the harvest. Also, the sailors had eaten a lot of precious food. This time they were greeted with much less enthusiasm. Within a few days, an argument broke out about the stealing of a rowboat; pandemonium erupted and Captain Cook was killed. Missionary Laura Judd, who visited Kealakekua Bay in 1829 and spoke with eyewitnesses, documented their accounts: "Women visited the ship in great numbers, and husbands grew jealous, and began to distrust these new divinities. . . . An old warrior said, 'I do not believe he is a god. I will prick him with my spear, and if he cries out I shall know he is not.' He struck him in the back, Cook uttered a cry, the chief gave another thrust, and the great navigator proved to be mortal."

In the British ship's chronicles, eye-witness Lieutenant King described what happened next: "On seeing him fall, the islanders set up a great shout, and his body was immediately dragged on shore, and surrounded by the enemy, who snatching daggers out of each other's hands, showed a savage eagerness to have a share in his destruction." Captain Cook's body was offered on Hikiau Heiau altar to the war god Kū. It was defleshed and the bones were respectfully wrapped in the manner accorded a chief's bones. Reports say that Cook's bones were for years ritually carried to harvest ceremonies around the island. One part of his body, however, came to a less dignified end: "I have seen the man who ate his heart," writes Judd. "He stole it from a tree, supposing it to be a swine's heart hung there to dry and was horrified when he discovered the truth. The Sandwich Islanders never were cannibals. This made him famous, and he is always spoken of as the man who ate Lono's heart."

This first contact between the Western World and Hawai'i was the beginning of great changes to the life and peoples of the Hawaiian Islands.

In the midst of Kealakekua Bay, a marble obelisk commemorates Captain James Cook.

Lahaina Village

The year 1819 was one of extraordinary events in the history of Hawai'i. It marked the death of the great Kamehameha I, the overthrow of the ancient code of sacred law known as the *kapu*, the arrival of the first whaling ships, and the imminent arrival of a shipload of New England missionaries. By 1823, the little town of Lahaina in west Maui was a bustling seaport and the whaling center of the world, humming with lusty whalers, romping seamen, nubile maidens, and zealous missionaries.

The first mission was established here by Reverend William Richards and his wife, puritanical young missionaries from New England who must have experienced quite a culture shock. The young couple immediately sought to impose a curfew on the drunken sailors and to stop native women from boarding the ships. They counted few successes until, one day, they suddenly acquired a powerful ally with the conversion of the regent Queen Ka'ahumanu to Christianity. On their advice, Queen Ka'ahumanu imposed the islands' first anti-sex laws. The laws attempted to cover all types of sexual conduct: one banned *Moe kolohe*, "sleeping around mischievously"; another was against "unnatural connection."

The seamen promptly rioted. Their captains

Historic whaling village of Lahaina

Banyan Tree Market

supported them, and a group of seamen armed with knives and pistols arrived at Reverend Richard's house. Mrs. Richards's, in the spirit of a martyr, flung herself between her husband and the seamen, telling the crowd that she was willing to lay down her life rather than "countenancing in the people we have come to enlighten, a course of conduct at variance with the word of God." At this, the Hawaiians joined the fray to save their beloved teacher.

By 1831, the missionaries had established the first American school in the islands. And the Hawaiians were eager students. One of the earliest students was David Malo, a brilliant young man who compiled the first book about pre-contact Hawai'i, *Mo'olelo Hawai'i* (Hawaiian Antiquities). This young convert loved his missionary teachers, but he realized that his native land was being taken over by the newcomers. In a letter of warning to the Hawaiian royalty, he wrote:

> . . .[T]he Ships of the white men have come, and smart people have arrived from the great Countries which you have never seen before, they know our people are few in number and living in a small country; they will eat us up, such has always been the case with large countries, the small ones have been gobbled up.

A self-guided walking tour of this historical seaside town, courtesy of the Lahaina Restoration Foundation, starts at the magnificent giant banyan tree at the corner of Hotel and Front Streets and leads to more than thirty historical sites, including the prison and courthouse in which Lahaina's rambunctious whalers and seamen spent many a night.

Waiola Church Cemetery

The small historic cemetery at Waiola Church in Lahaina, Maui, holds the graves of both Hawaiian royalty and Westerners, such as missionary William Richards. The inscriptions on the old tombstones of Queen Keōpūolani and her daughter, Princess Nahiʻenaʻena, give no indication of the turbulent lives of these two women, who lived at a time when two worlds collided. Nor do they tell the story of Princess Nahiʻenaʻena and her brother, two star-crossed lovers.

While still a baby, Princess Nahiʻenaʻena was betrothed to her brother, Prince Kauikeaouli. This was a *naha* union, blessed by the gods, to preserve the sanctity of the bloodline—but a union that would be looked on aghast by the coming missionaries. Nahiʻenaʻena's mother would eventually embrace the Christian faith, and her dying wish was that her daughter be educated and brought up "like the wives of the missionaries." The missionaries took the little princess to their hearts and renamed her Princess Harriet.

But Princess Nahiʻenaʻena still loved her brother, and she looked forward to marrying him as the fulfillment of her sacred role. Also, the young girl found life at court fun and exciting. Her prince, now King Kamehameha III, lived a merry life of wild parties and heavy drinking, of which the missionaries of course disapproved. Confused, Nahiʻenaʻena fluctuated between royal life with her brother and her wish to please her missionary teachers and to attain salvation.

The elder Hawaiian chiefs decided to solve the problem themselves. Nahiʻenaʻena and Kamehameha III were married according to ancient Hawaiian custom: by sleeping together in the presence of the chiefs. The missionaries were appalled. Reverend Richards wrote to Nahiʻenaʻena from her mother's grave, deploring the marriage and telling her to return from Honolulu to Lahaina.

Eventually, the truculent princess obeyed her teacher. But she returned so defiant and her behavior was so bad that Reverend Richards threatened her with excommunication. The missionaries quickly arranged for her marriage to a young chief. Nahiʻenaʻena lived with her new husband in Lahaina, but paid long visits to her brother in Honolulu. When Nahiʻenaʻena became pregnant, her brother, the king, declared that he alone was the ultimate law and came to take his sister back to Honolulu for the royal birth. They spent four happy months together leading, according to missionary Laura Judd, "a high life." Nahiʻenaʻena gave birth to a son, but the baby died. The tragic young princess died a few months later.

Nahiʻenaʻena was laid to rest beside her mother in a mausoleum on the royal island in Mokuhina Pond in Lahaina. Her brother had a thatched home built beside the mausoleum so that he could spend time near his beloved sister. After her death, he became a sober and respected ruler. The Hawaiian people considered Nahiʻenaʻena's death a sacrifice and named the street of her funeral procession Luakini (Sacrifice) Street. Later, when the royal island was being demolished in order to develop modern Lahaina, the bodies of Keōpūolani and Nahiʻenaʻena were moved to Waiola Church Cemetery.

Kalaupapa Peninsula

The Kalaupapa Peninsula, a long tongue of lava, reaches out into the swirling seas below the dark, high sea cliffs of Moloka'i. The peninsula is one of the most isolated spots in the Hawaiian Islands, accessible only by a long switchback trail that runs down a 1,700-foot-high cliff, via the perilous seas, or by helicopter. The peninsula found its way into Hawaiian history in 1866, when leprosy was discovered in the islands. Those who contracted the dreaded disease were rounded up, loaded onto a ship, and sent to Kalaupapa. The Royal Board of Health optimistically thought that the patients would be able to support themselves by fishing and working the land.

When the first boatload of sick people anchored in the choppy bay at Kalawao, they were told to jump into the ocean and make their own way to the shore. The frightened sailors kept their distance, but they flung a few sealed barrels of food and clothing after the floundering people. Those too sick to swim simply drowned, and once on shore, the weak fell prey to the strong. Between 1866 and 1874, 1,145 lepers were sent to the colony. Boatloads of new sufferers were greeted with this phrase of despair: "In this place, there is no law." The Hawaiian monarchy eventually established a hospital, but in reality there was very little help and every type of crime.

In 1873, a young Catholic priest, Father Damien, arrived from Belgium. His mission in life was to give succor to the lepers. He lived with them, fed them, bathed their wounds, and built shelters with his own hands. Eventually he, too, contracted leprosy. His congregation knew that he had been infected when he started a sermon, "We lepers . . ." Robert Louis Stevenson visited Kalaupapa shortly after Father Damien's death in 1880. Writing about him in his "Open Letter" to the Reverend Dr. Hyde, Stevenson says: "At a blow, and with the price of his life, he made the place illustrious and public. If ever a man brought reforms, and died to bring them, it was he. It brought money, public interest, and best of all, it brought personal and caring supervision in the form of Brother Joseph Dutton and the Sisters of the Franciscan Convent of St. Anthony of Syracuse, New York."

Today, there are still residents in the small town of Kalaupapa. The population has dwindled to less than 40 elderly patients, all of whom have been cleared of leprosy, now called Hansen's Disease. They are free to leave anytime they wish, and occasionally they travel to another island—sometimes even to Las Vegas. However, leaving Kalaupapa can be scary for people who have lived there most of their lives, and many who try life outside wind up returning to the isolation they call home.

Mission Houses Museum

We share each other's woes
Our mutual burdens bear,
And often for each other flows
The sympathizing tear…
　　　—From "Blest Be the Tie that Binds," John
　　　　　　　　　　　　　　　Fawcett, 1782

Relics of a bygone time, the islands' first mission houses are a cluster of small, white buildings that stand in shady gardens in the center of downtown Honolulu. The wooden frame structure for the main house was brought precut from Boston in 1819 by the first missionaries. Many missionary families occupied it over the years; sometimes as many as four families lived in the small house at the same time. In spite of Hawai'i's warm weather, the windows were fixed closed in the New England style.

In contrast to the Hawaiians, who wore minimal clothing—if any at all—the missionary men always wore their long underwear, and the missionary women wore petticoats, long-sleeved blouses, and bonnets. The clothing issue created some interesting incidents: Voluptuous Queen Ka'ahumanu visited the missionaries one day after an ocean swim and sat naked on the sofa with "ease and self-possession," chatting. The missionaries didn't know quite where to look as she came, in the words of Lucy Thurston, "as if from Eden, in the dress of innocence."

Missionary annals relate how, every evening, a crowd of Hawaiians would assemble outside and peer into the kitchen to watch the "long necks" cook. Later, more would gather at the open door to watch the men and women sit down and eat together, a custom the Hawaiians found bizarre because sacred law forbade men and women to eat together. Eventually, the beleaguered missionaries closed the door and cut two windows that they draped.

Next to the main house stands the printing house. The missionaries were young, energetic, and devoted to their cause of converting the pagan. They immediately began the daunting task of learning the lilting, confusingly vowel-rich, only-oral Hawaiian language, and they just as soon put it into visual form, creating a written Hawaiian alphabet with five vowels and seven consonants. From there, the New Testament Book of Matthew, textbooks, and biblical tracts in the Hawaiian language were printed on a printing press brought from New England. It took eight hours of hard work to set up one page, but the magic of the printed word fascinated the Hawaiians. Even Queen Ka'ahumanu became interested in learning to read, and the great mass of the chiefs and Hawaiians eagerly followed and attended the mission schools. By 1840, Hawaii had officially become a Christian nation, and it boasted higher literacy than any contemporary country.

Kawaiaha'o Church

Kawaiaha'o Church, named for the "Waters of Ha'o," a nearby sacred spring, is the oldest remaining church in Honolulu. Reverend Hiram Bingham drew up the plans for the church, and between 1837 and 1842, it was constructed from more than 14,000 coral blocks quarried by Hawaiian divers from reefs ten to twenty feet deep in the ocean. In 1837, missionary Laura Judd wrote of the process: "The walls of the king's chapel are commenced, and many natives are employed in cutting and dragging coral stones from the seashore. It is a Herculean task to perform this work without beasts of burden, or the aid of any labor-saving machinery."

A large and festive service was held here in 1843, when the British returned the Hawaiian Islands to Hawaiian sovereignty after a brief period of unwanted and mostly unintended

British rule. King Kamehameha III gave thanks at the ceremony with the words destined to become the motto of the Hawaiian Islands: "The life of the land is preserved in righteousness."

The small mausoleum outside the church holds the body of King Lunalilo. When his mother, who was not considered as royal as the Kamehameha family, was refused burial in the Royal Mausoleum in Nu'uanu Valley, the king announced that he had no desire to be buried there either and wished to be buried near his beloved mother at Kawaiaha'o Church.

Newspaper reports at the time of Lunalilo's death relate that thunder boomed like a twenty-one gun salute on the night of the king's burial.

Sunday services at Kawaiaha'o Church are in Hawaiian and English, and are highlighted by Hawaiian hymns. The church is also still the site of pageantry, when, for example, Hawaiian societies march in regalia wearing long black cloaks and feather leis and waving tall feathered standards to honor royal forebears, who are commemorated by plaques and portraits on the church's walls.

Wai'oli Mission House

Nestled in Kaua'i's green Hanalei Valley beneath fantastical mountain spires, this two-story white mission house with wide verandas was part of a small settlement of church, school, and homes built piece by piece by New England missionaries. The house was lovingly restored in 1921 by the resident granddaughters of two of the home's former residents, missionaries Abner and Lucy Wilcox, who moved into the house in 1846.

In the parlor, Lucy Wilcox taught Hawaiian girls to sew. In the kitchen, she churned butter and baked breads and cakes in the chimney-side oven. Shelves hold books brought by the family. Letters written by Reverend Wilcox bring the family to life as he worries about his sons and, writing while on a visit to faraway Connecticut, assures Lucy that her family and friends miss her and have sewn a quilt with patches embossed with the family name.

Nearby are the funky, laid back little town of Hanalei, with its eclectic collection of green clapboard-and-shingle stores and restaurants; the wide Hanalei River; and the beautiful, crescent-shaped Hanalei Bay—which is, according to the song, the home of Puff, the Magic Dragon.

Left: Wai'oli Mission House church

Parker Ranch

The 225,000-acre Parker Ranch is one of the country's oldest ranches, and it was once the largest private ranch under single ownership in the United States. Here, in Waimea on the Big Island of Hawai'i, 55,000 cattle graze in impossibly green pastures, wreathed in mountain mists and occasional vog (a mixture of fog and volcanic steam).

In 1809, just one generation after Captain Cook first arrived in Hawai'i, 19-year-old John Parker, a sailor and the son of a Massachusetts ship owner, arrived on a ship seeking sandalwood. He noted that the forests were quickly being diminished and wondered what would fuel the island economy when the sandalwood was gone. The sight of the lush plains captivated him. He learned that thousands of maverick cattle roamed Hawai'i's remote valleys, offspring of the five head of cattle given to Kamehameha I by Captain Vancouver some 20 years earlier. Detecting the scent of opportunity, John Parker jumped ship.

A restless youth, Parker left for a spell of adventuring in China, but returned to Hawai'i in 1812. He established a relationship with Kamehameha I based on mutual respect and was the first man given the privilege of permission to shoot some of the islands' maverick cattle. After a time, salt beef began to replace sandalwood as the chief export from Hawai'i—mostly due to Parker's efforts. Parker married the daughter of a high chief, and as the family grew, so did the maverick herds. When the cattle became thick and dangerous, Kamehameha III sent to California for vaqueros, Spanish-Mexican cowboys, to teach the Hawaiians how to work the ranges. The colorful cowboys, with their wide sombreros, ornate hand-sewn saddles, and flashing spurs, fascinated the islanders. The first three to arrive became instant celebrities known to the natives as "paniolo," derived from the word "español."

In 1845, Kamehameha III allowed Parker to buy two acres of land for the token payment of ten dollars cash. In the Great Mahele, when the king divided up Hawai'i's lands between the chiefs, Parker's wife, the daughter of a high-ranking chief, received 680 acres. From these lands, hard work and determination forged the immense Parker Ranch.

The cowboys, or paniolo, are the backbone of Parker Ranch. They resemble the classic figures of the American West, but with a tropical twist. On their wide-brimmed hats they sometimes sport a garland of flowers. Their frontier is Mauna Kea, one of the world's highest volcanoes, and their range sweeps from sea cliffs across stark volcanic ranges and over lush pastures. In the early history of the ranch, these paniolo shipped cattle to market by swimming them out to boats offshore. Leading the steer with his rope, the mounted paniolo would muscle the panic-stricken animal through the surf and lash it to the side of the longboats. A winch with a sling then hoisted the steer onto the deck of an inter-island steamer. The entire operation was extremely dangerous, both for the frightened cattle and the paniolo. Today, rodeos at the Parker Ranch provide a close-up look at a close-knit and gracious Hawaiian community working and playing together as it has for many generations.

Sugar Cane Fields

Fields of rippling sugar cane cover the foothills and plains of central Kaua'i, the remains of the area's once-vibrant sugar industry. Sugar cane was brought to Hawai'i in the canoes of the first Polynesian arrivals and was growing wild when Captain Cook arrived in 1778. It became a major crop on the four largest Hawaiian Islands, but not without a struggle.

The main problem for the sugar cane plantations was labor: Hawaiians quickly realized that this was very hard work for very little pay, and they simply left the fields at every opportunity or refused to work at all. The plantation owners turned to Asia for workers, particularly from China, Japan, and later Portugal, the Philippines, and Korea. They attempted to play nationalities off against each other to reduce the likelihood of labor disputes, as the Planters' Monthly declared: "By employing different nationalities, there is less danger of collusion among laborers and the employers." Though they came from different places, the migrants soon shared many experiences: the long sea voyage in steerage, homesickness, and the demanding work. In the book *Pau Hāna*, a Korean worker recalls the long hours she spent cutting cane:

> The sugar cane fields were endless and (the stalks) were twice the height of myself. Now that I look back, I thank goodness for the height, for if I had seen how far the fields stretched, I probably would have fainted from knowing how much work was ahead. My waistline got slimmer and my back ached from bending over all the time to cut sugar cane.

The son of a sugarcane worker, Milton Murayama, wrote a book about his family's experiences in the cane fields entitled *All I Asking For Is My Body*. The title says it all.

Despite their hardships, the migrants were resilient and their spirits were indomitable. Although they usually intended to return home when their contracts terminated, most remained on the islands. Today, Hawai'i's society of diverse cultures and ethnic groups owes its roots to the plantation workers. A song quoted in Pau Hāna tells quite simply how it happened:

> *With one woven basket*
> *Alone I came*
> *Now I have children*
> *And even grandchildren too.*

A tree tunnel of tall swamp mahogany trees leads to Kōloa, the first plantation town, established in 1835 around the original sugar cane fields and still involved in sugar cane production. Huge monkeypod trees canopy the quaint clapboard storefronts, wooden houses, and three picturesque and still-thriving temples that offer a glimpse into early plantation life.

Tucked beneath the canopy are the remnants of Kōloa Sugar Mill,
Hawai'i's first successful sugar mill, established 1835.

Pineapple Plantations

James Dole started growing pineapples on a 20-acre farm in Wahiwā, Oʻahu, in the early 1900s. He was so successful that, by 1920, Hawaiʻi was the largest producer of pineapples in the world. Oʻahu became a major producer, and the whole island of Lānaʻi turned into one giant pineapple plantation.

Work in the pineapple plantations was intense, and soon plantation owners began bringing in migrant workers. Noting that married Japanese men worked much longer hours than single Filipinos, the planters concluded that men with families were steadier workers than single men. They began encouraging their workers to seek brides back home by participating in a picture bride arrangement. Pau Hāna, a book on plantation life by a Korean laborer, relates that pictures sent back home to secure brides were not always recent. A bride in the book recalls how startled she was when she met her future husband, "When I see him, he skinny and black. I no like. No look like picture. But no can go home."

Life for the immigrants was hard, but over the years Hawai'i became home. Workers brought their customs, traditions, and foods to the new land and developed a unique working-class culture in the camps. They ensured that their children were educated, and those children of yesterday's plantation workers became the government officials, schoolteachers, businessmen, and professionals of Hawai'i today.

Route 99 leading to O'ahu's North Shore passes through miles of pineapple fields, and a display plot at the intersection of Route 80 showcases the different varieties of the fruit. Nearby Dole Pineapple Plantation sells all types of pineapples and pineapple creations, including mouth-watering pineapple ice cream.

In the center of the vast pineapple fields, a sacred site, Kūkaniloko Birthing Stones, is a fascinating reminder of ancient Hawai'i. Here, on large, bowl-shaped lava rocks, royal mothers gave birth to the powerful chiefs of long ago. The birthing stones were also said to be fertility stones—a powerful reputation that lives on. Women desiring children still leave offerings there: flower leis and small, sweet pineapples from the adjacent fields.

'Iolani Palace

Coat of arms of the Hawaiian Kingdom, with the motto "The life of the land is perpetuated in righteousness."

*While humbly meditating
Within these walls imprisoned
Thou art my light, my haven
Thy glory my support.*

*Oh look not on their failings
Nor on the sins of men
Forgive with loving kindness
That we might be made pure.*
—from "Queen's Prayer," by Queen Lili'uokalani, 1895

In Honolulu, a wide, palm-lined driveway leads from King Street through elaborate wrought-iron gates and park-like grounds to 'Iolani Palace. *'Io* is the Hawaiian hawk, the bird that flies higher than the rest, and *lani* means heavenly or exalted. The palace was the official residence of Hawa'i's two last monarchs, King Kalākaua, who ruled from 1874 until his death in 1891, and his sister, Queen Lili'uokalani, who reigned from 1891 until the overthrow of the Hawaiian monarchy in 1893.

The lives of Hawai'i's last monarchs were filled with the drama and excitement of an epic novel. King Kalākaua, the "Merrie Monarch," built 'Iolani Palace in 1882; the Italian Renaissance design was inspired by his European travels. Intrigued by new technology, the king installed the most innovative devices of the age, such as indoor plumbing, sinks with running water, electric lights, and telephones. Electric lights were shining at the palace only seven years after Edison perfected the first incandescent light bulb—that's even before electricity was installed at the White House.

At the king's coronation ceremony at 'Iolani Palace, he raised his crown to his head in Napoleonic fashion and also crowned his consort, Queen Kapi'olani. Some 8,000 Hawaiians cheered, but foreign businessmen boycotted the event, a sign of their dissatisfaction with the monarch and of the troubled times to come. A storm was gathering over the monarchy that would break after Kalākaua's death in 1891, when his sister Lili'uokalani ascended the throne. Lili'uokalani would soon face a formidable threat to the monarchy and to the independence of the kingdom.

An intelligent and strong-minded woman, Lili'uokalani felt that the United States had too much influence over Hawai'i. She planned to replace the liberal "Bayonet" constitution forced on her brother by business interests with an autocratic mandate giving the monarchy political and economic control. This drew her into heated conflict with the plantation owners, who saw her as an obstacle to their economic growth and favored the annexation of the islands to the democratic United States.

January 17, 1893 was a day of bloodless revolution. With upheaval in her own cabinet, hundreds of native Hawaiians and royalists gathered at Palace Square, and armed troops from an American warship marching past the palace, Queen Lili'iuokalani yielded her throne to avoid bloodshed. She believed that the United States government would investigate the facts and reinstate her. In the meantime, a provisional government was established. As the queen had hoped, the Cleveland Administration rejected the annexation and requested that the provisional government restore the monarchy. The provisional government flatly refused to comply; in 1894, it became the Republic of Hawai'i, and its leader, Sanford B. Dole, became president.

From the beginning, the new government was nervous about a royalist uprising. 'Iolani Palace was sandbagged and garrisoned. In 1895, a brief counter-revolution failed, and a cache of weapons was discovered in Queen Lili'uokalani's garden at Washington Place. She denied knowledge of a royalist plot. 'Iolani Palace's glittering

throne room, where so many lavish parties once were held, became the military court where Liliʻuokalani was tried on treason-related charges. The queen was placed under house arrest in a bedroom on the second floor of the palace. Finally, she abdicated and swore allegiance to the new republic. In 1896, she was released and returned to her home at Washington Place, where she lived for two decades, remaining "queen" to the Hawaiians who loved her. Her glorious palace was converted into government offices.

In 1898, the Republic of Hawaiʻi became a U.S. Territory, and in 1959 it became the fiftieth state of the United States of America. When a new capitol building was constructed in 1969, the decision was made to restore ʻIolani Palace to its former glory. Today, visitors wearing borrowed slippers to protect the gleaming koa wood floors can take guided tours through the palace—the only true royal palace in the United States.

Above: Façade of ʻIolani Palace.

Below: ʻIolani Barracks, constructed of coral blocks in 1871.

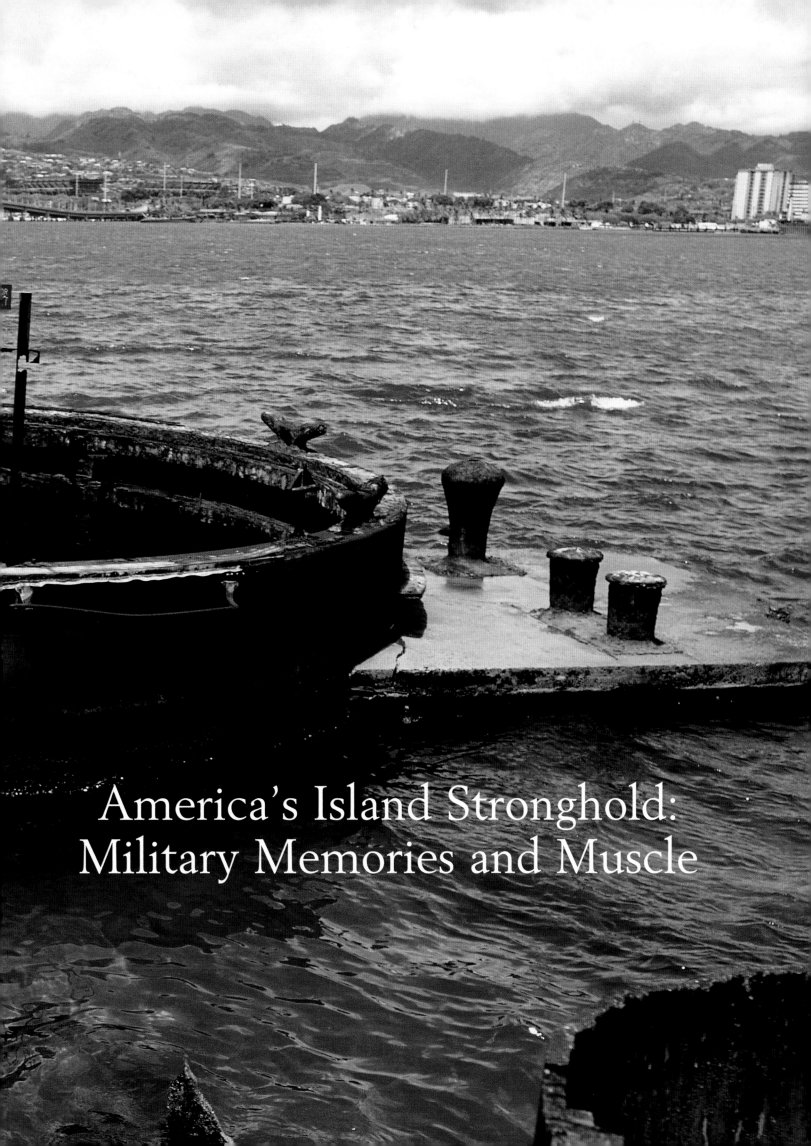

America's Island Stronghold:
Military Memories and Muscle

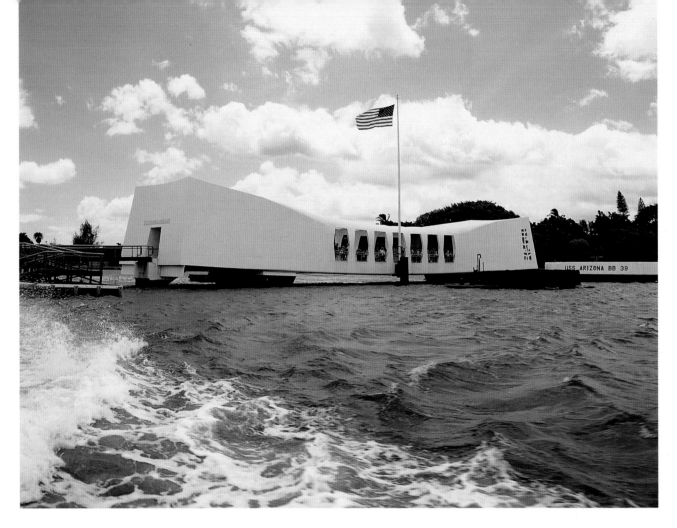

USS Arizona Memorial

Yesterday, December 7, 1941—a date which will live in infamy—the United States of America was suddenly and deliberately attacked by naval and air forces of the empire of Japan.
—Franklin Delano Roosevelt

In O'ahu's Pearl Harbor, a brilliant white shrine spans the sunken hull of the USS *Arizona*, the mighty battleship and tomb of over 1,000 men. The attack on the *Arizona* and America's Pacific Fleet at Pearl Harbor caused such massive loss of life that this single event convinced the United States to enter World War II.

On a quiet Sunday morning, December 7, 1941, over the island of O'ahu, two waves of Japanese fighter planes broke through the cloud cover. They dive-bombed, torpedoed, and strafed the docked American battleships of the Pacific Fleet, sinking or seriously damaging 20 ships, destroying 350 planes, and killing 2,335 American servicemen—the largest single loss in

United States history. Pearl Harbor had been dredged some 40 years before to accommodate the largest of the U.S. warships. Now it was the scene of the nation's greatest military disaster.

In the aftermath of the attack, a crack team of U.S. Navy salvage divers was charged with the Herculean task of bringing up the bodies of the dead, salvaging the ships, and resurrecting the pride of the Pacific Fleet. In his book *Descent Into Darkness*, Commander Edward C. Rayner tells how navy divers entered the interiors of sunken battleships, a world of total blackness, where sediment and oil made diving lamps useless. Using only their sense of feel, the divers groped through hundreds of feet inside the ships to their work assignments, making repairs and salvaging vital war materials. They coped with sharks, the eerie presence of the victims, and unseen dangers. Some of the divers were killed; others were severely injured.

Nevertheless, the divers accomplished their

Previous page: A portion of the original USS Arizona, *sunk in the 1941 attack on Pearl Harbor.*

goal with enormous success. The raised ships were dry-docked at the Pearl Harbor Naval Shipyard and sent out to be repaired, overhauled, and modernized. Of the 20 U.S. vessels that went down that day, 17 rose to fight again. The USS *Helena* returned to strike at Guadalcanal. The USS *Nevada* came back to settle its score with the Japanese at Iwo Jima and Okinawa. After being salvaged, the USS *West Virginia* won five battle stars in 12 months, then steamed into Tokyo Bay on September 1, 1945. There it anchored alongside the USS *Missouri*, where Douglas MacArthur waited to accept the Japanese surrender, and witnessed the final interment of the enemy that had tried to end its days.

At the memorial's visitors' center on shore, a short film shows the maiden voyage of the USS *Arizona* and poignant scenes of happy, young seamen on shore-leave in Honolulu. Nearby are displayed photographs, historic documents, and personal mementos of the seamen. From the visitors' center, U.S. Navy launches take visitors to the memorial shrine, where a heartbreaking list of the names of the 1,177 men who went down with the USS *Arizona* is engraved on a marble wall. Visitors often throw leis into the water, and purple orchids float about the seawater-corroded superstructure of the ship that rises above the waves. Oil still oozes slowly up from the *Arizona*'s engine room, staining the pristine blue Pacific. The USS *Arizona* is the only sunken ship that remains a commissioned vessel of the U.S. Navy, and passing warships still render naval honors to her and to those who died.

USS Missouri

One of the largest battleships ever built, the 58,000-ton, 200-foot-tall USS *Missouri*, is docked on "Battleship Row," Ford Island, near the USS *Arizona* in Pearl Harbor. The attack on the USS *Arizona* and the other ships at Pearl Harbor by Japanese pilots brought the United States into the war with the Japanese and the Germans. It was on the deck of the USS *Missouri* that the Japanese later surrendered to the United States, bringing World War II to an end.

Commissioned in 1944, the "Mighty Mo" provided gunfire support for bombing raids over Tokyo and firepower in the battles of Iwo Jima and Okinawa, and later participated in several bombardments during the Korean conflict. In 1955, the battleship was decommissioned and retired to Puget Sound Naval Shipyard in Washington. Then, in 1986, the ship was modernized and sent back into action. Shortly before its final decommission in 1992, it was deployed in the Persian Gulf, where it participated in Tomahawk strike missions and land bombardments during Operation Desert

The largest guns the U.S. Navy has ever made at 16 inches in diameter

Storm. In 1998, Hawai'i won the battle to keep this living legend in Pearl Harbor beside the USS *Arizona* Memorial.

The USS *Missouri's* main battery consists of three massive gun turrets, each holding three 65-foot-long guns—some of the biggest floating guns on earth. During the 1986 remodernization, the ship was outfitted with sixteen Harpoon anti-ship missiles with a range of 75 miles, each with a 500-pound warhead, as well as eight Tomahawk Armored Box Launchers holding a total of 32 missiles. The addition of the latter extended the ship's striking distance to over 1,000 miles!

National Memorial Cemetery of the Pacific

In proud remembrance of the achievements of her sons and in humble tribute to their sacrifices this memorial has been erected by the United States of America.

—Inscription on the chapel vestibule at the National Memorial Cemetery of the Pacific

Pūowaina (Hill of Sacrifice) is the ancient Hawaiian name for Punchbowl Crater in the heart of Honolulu. The name was prophetic: the green and peaceful crater now holds the National Memorial Cemetery of the Pacific, one of the world's greatest tributes to selfless sacrifice. Thousands of marble slabs and plaques here mark the resting places of more than 33,000 men and women who made the ultimate sacrifice.

The crater holds a strategic position high over Honolulu. When World War II broke out in the Pacific, guns were placed here to defend Oʻahu from a possible attack. It was presumed that the attack would come from the sea; when Japan attacked from the air, the United States was caught off its guard and thousands died at Pearl Harbor. Bodies were brought to Honolulu and kept in mausoleum warehouses. In 1949, the first burial service took place at the National Memorial Cemetery of the Pacific, and for the first time the bugle calls of "Taps" echoed hauntingly across the crater.

Today, more than five million visitors pay their tributes each year: the annual sunrise Easter service alone draws thousands, and on Veterans' Day the crater is ablaze with flower leis and flags. In pilgrim-like silence, visitors climb the steps to the monument and walk slowly through the Courts of the Missing, where marble slabs are engraved with the names of nearly thirty thousand MIAs whose bodies have never been recovered. Huge battle maps list the names that resound in the American memory: Pearl Harbor, Wake, Midway, Iwo Jima, Coral Sea, Gilbert Islands, Okinawa . . .

View of Honolulu from Diamond Head

Diamond Head

Craggy Diamond Head, a volcanic cone in Honolulu, won its name when nineteenth-century British sailors discovered calcite crystals on its slopes and, for some jubilant moments, mistook them for diamonds. But long before the Brits arrived, the ancient Hawaiians built at least seven major temples and smaller fishing shrines on Diamond Head, and when Kamehameha the

Great conquered Oʻahu, he held a formal ceremony —with all the usual human sacrifices—at the greatest of those temples. The summit of Diamond Head was also used as a lookout for menacing fleets of war canoes; for friendly visitors coming from outer islands, a bonfire was kept alight there.

Much later, the U.S. Government would recognize the advantage of strengthening coastal defenses on Oʻahu, and in 1904 purchased Diamond Head to develop a military reservation. The site became a coastal defense fort, with guns poking out from the rocks on its high walls. Fort Ruger, built inside the crater, housed cannon mortars with a range of eleven miles and a telescope station for sighting targets. A series of tunnels provided access to the crater floor, and in 1910 a trail was carved by hand and shovel leading up the interior of the crater to the observation site at the top. Its apparent impenetrability earned Diamond Head the nickname "Gibraltar of the Pacific."

None of the site's fortifications was ever put to use during World War I, but after the U.S. entered World War II, the military installations at Diamond Head became top secret. The old military observation point was replaced by radar equipment, and anti-aircraft guns were added; still, none of these was ever fired in battle. In 1950, the military removed all weaponry from Diamond Head, and use of the crater passed to the National Guard.

Today, Diamond Head is no longer a restricted military facility, but a state park that boasts over one million visitors a year. A well-marked trail leads three-quarters of a mile along switchbacks, up four sets of narrow stairways, then through a series of pitch-dark tunnels to the observation station at the top of the crater. There, hikers get a bird's eye view of Oʻahu's south shore, the plains of central Oʻahu, the Koʻolau Mountains, and the sparkling Pacific.

Diamond Head Lighthouse, built in 1917, is still in service today.

H-3 Interstate

While interstates on the American continent generally connect states, Oʻahu's massive interstates connect the multitude of military bases scattered all over the island. The H-3 is one of three highways in Oʻahu that were funded by the federal government because of their designation as defense highways. Completed in 1997, the H-3 links Hickam Air Force Base and the Marine Corp Base Hawaiʻi Kāneʻohe. The highway is not only of military importance, though: it also connects Leeward and Windward Oʻahu, making it one of the nation's most spectacular mountain drives. For 16 miles, the road tunnels through volcanic mountains and soars across long viaducts over incredibly lush valleys. It took 37 years and $3 billion to overcome the unusual challenges posed by the island's unique geology, climate, and cultural heritage. Not least among them was the breathtaking scenery itself, which forced engineers to consider the traffic hazards posed by motorists who would surely slow down—or stop altogether —just to get a better look!

Niʻihau

Niʻihau is called the "Forbidden Island," an irresistible name to any curious traveler. The entire island is privately owned by the Robinsons, a family from New Zealand who purchased it from Kamehameha IV for $10,000 in 1864. (Originally, the king offered to sell a beach called Waikīkī, but the Robinsons chose Niʻihau instead.) The family established a sheep and cattle ranch there, declaring that nothing would ever change the island. This wish has gone largely fulfilled: most of the tiny island—including even the ocean around it to a distance of 60 feet from shore—is off-limits to everyone but its 230 native Hawaiian residents. Residents are free to come and go as they wish, but they still prefer to remain fishers and farmers on Niʻihau, living much as they would have two centuries ago. Helicopter tours take visitors on a three-hour excursion to the Forbidden Island, visiting two isolated beaches. To visit the residents, one needs a personal invitation.

The finest shell necklaces in Hawaiʻi come from Niʻihau. During the three-month "shell season," many residents spend all the daylight hours sifting sand and gathering the tiny, rare Niʻihau shells. The shells are finely drilled and painstakingly strung into exquisite white, pink, and yellow necklaces that sell for hundreds and even thousands of dollars in Waikīkī stores. Called "the Gems of the Pacific," these tiny treasures with a distinctive sheen are the only shell jewelry in the world that can be insured with an appraisal from a licensed appraiser, just like any other precious gem.

Because of its long-forbidden status, most visitors to Hawaiʻi never realize that they're missing an important piece of World War II history here. On the morning of December 7, 1941, a Japanese pilot landed his damaged plane on a Niʻihau field. The people of the tiny island ran to help him, unaware that he had just bombed Pearl Harbor. After several days of practically holding the islanders hostage, the pilot shot Ben Kanehele, a strapping native Hawaiian, in the stomach, groin, and thigh. (Later, Ben would say, "That's when I got mad.") Bleeding profusely from his wounds, Ben picked up the pilot and brained him against a stone wall—effectively ending the Battle for Niʻihau. A new saying came out of the victory, "Don't shoot a Hawaiian three times or you'll make him mad."

The Navy's unmanned radar installation can barely be seen atop this cliff on the east side of Niʻihau.

Sun, Sand, Surf . . . and Sophistication: Hawai'i Today

Dancers celebrating *King Kamehameha Day (June 11)* on the island of O'ahu.

Right: On the island of O'ahu, the statue of King Kamehameha is covered with leis for King Kamehameha Day (June 11).

Hawaiian Holidays

May Day is Lei Day in Hawai'i
Garlands of flowers everywhere
Oh, all the colors in the rainbow
Maidens with blossoms in their hair
Flowers that mean we should be happy
Throwing aside our load of care
Oh, May Day is Lei Day in Hawai'i
Lei Day is happy day out there.
　　—"May Day is Lei Day in Hawai'i," by Leonard "Red" Hawk, 1928

Festivals and feasts, pageants and parades, flower and firework shows, rodeos, river races, and religious ceremonies abound in Hawai'i. The people of the Hawaiian Islands love a good festival, and they celebrate all the

Previous page: Kailua Beach

Pāʻū *riders celebrate King Kamehameha Day (June 11) on the island of Oʻahu.*

American national holidays in addition to their own multi-cultural celebrations and ethnic events. The Aloha Festival is the state's largest multi-ethnic event. Every year from the beginning of September to the end of October, all the islands celebrate *aloha* (love) with various entertainments, including *luʻau* (feasts) and parades with costumed participants riding flower-bedecked floats.

The stars of the Aloha Festival, as well as of King Kamehameha Day (June 11), are the *pāʻū* riders. Representing the different islands, these native Hawaiians on horseback are clad in elaborate skirts of satin and velvet similar to those worn by *pāʻū* riders a hundred years ago. Around their necks and in their hair, riders wear fragrant flower leis, and their glossy horses are also bedecked in flowers, bright berries, and woven leaf leis.

Other unique Hawaiian holidays observed on all the islands include Lei Day (May 1) festivals, which are particularly appealing at the schools, where bright-eyed pupils wear flower leis around their necks and the sweet smell of plumeria flowers fill the air; Buddha Day (closest Sunday to April 8th), on which kimono-clad Japanese islanders celebrate the birthday of Buddha with sunrise ceremonies at Kapiʻolani Park, Oʻahu, and with flower festivals, pageants, and dances at island temples; and Chinese New Year, when fire-crackers chase evil spirits out of Chinatown so that the neighborhood's children can enjoy the holiday's fierce dragons and thousands of glowing lanterns.

Mauna Kea Golf Course

L ong ago, mighty Hawaiian chiefs came to the Kohala Coast on the Big Island of Hawai'i to relax and get away from the pressures of war and conquest. Today, visitors come to the area's many luxury resorts to relax, swim, surf, and play golf. Hawai'i has been named a "golf heaven," with perfect weather and a variety of courses. Golf Magazine even gave the Gold Medal Award to three Hawaiian resorts, ranking them among the 12 best resorts in America.

One of the islands' most famous greens is no doubt the 18-hole championship golf course at the lavish Mauna Kea Resort complex. Visitors who have seen its breathtaking beauty find it hard to believe that architect Robert Trent Jones Sr. created these undulating greens right on top of a wasteland of solid black lava rock. The result is almost as challenging to play as it was to design: Hawai'i's most famous and most photographed hole, Mauna Kea's number 3, is rated among the "100 Best Holes in the World" by Golf Digest. A par there requires a strong, 145-yard tee shot over the Pacific Ocean to a green that's 60 yards deep and protected by bunkers.

Dolphin Lagoon at the Hilton Waikoloa Village

In the fantasy world of the Hilton Waikoloa Village in South Kohala on the Big Island of Hawai'i, visitors glide in mahogany boats along winding canals past perfumed gardens and priceless art treasures from Hawai'i, Oceania, and Asia. Others zip on a silver monorail from restaurants to pools, past thundering waterfalls and tranquil grottoes. Even more fortunate guests get to take part in a real-life fantasy: a swim in a saltwater lagoon with the resort's most popular residents, the dolphins.

Adults are chosen from a lottery drawn on a daily basis; kids are much luckier: with two months' advance booking, all of them may participate. In addition to being loads of fun, Dolphin Quest is an educational experience that teaches people about these intelligent and friendly sea creatures. Swimmers spend forty-five minutes in the pool, first getting acquainted with the dolphins and then swimming around with them, all the while learning about the animals and marine conservation from the dolphins' caretakers. The program was developed with the intention of preserving and protecting dolphin populations, and much of the proceeds goes toward marine research.

In their 2.5 million-gallon blue lagoon, the dolphins are the hosts. They stop if they want to be petted, or zoom by like torpedoes if there's something else they'd rather do. The smiling dolphins who do participate seem to enjoy it, but for the human participants, this is an extraordinarily unusual and wonderful experience—few things can compete with stroking the tummy of a baby dolphin and feeling the thud of its heartbeat.

Author, Ellie, and husband, Will, delight in holding Kei, a baby dolphin

Whale Watching

Humpback whales, as big as a bus and weighing in at some 80,000 pounds, leap and spin gracefully off the coast of Maui, waving their flukes, diving, and snorting great geysers of water into the air. Visitors to Hawai'i from late November to early May have an excellent chance of spotting them. Perhaps the best way to spot a whale from the shore is to watch for its "spout," the high fountain of air and spray forced from the whale's blowhole—the reason whalers used to shout "Thar she blows!"

Female whales migrate to Hawaii to calve in the warm protected waters of the Hawaiian Islands Humpback Whale National Marine Sanctuary. Migration peaks in February, when the whales congregate mostly in the coastal waters of Maui to feed their 3,000-pound newborn calves until the latter are fat enough for the 3,500-mile swim north. After calving comes mating, when of course the male whales follow the females. A hot pursuit is an important part of whale mating, as it ensures that only the fittest males will mate with a female. During mating season, the ocean echoes with the strange sound of whale songs. All the singing whales know the song and sing it again and again, but the "hit song" stays on the charts for only one year—still much longer than most human top hits. The humpback's song is said to be the loudest and most complex vocalization in the animal kingdom. Why the whales sing remains a mystery.

It's impossible to comprehend just how gigantic these giants of the deep truly are until one sees them close up from a boat. Safety regulations require whale-viewing boats to stay a hundred yards away from the whales, but the whales don't always obey the rules. When a great humpback with a gaping mouth that could easily swallow a Volkswagen swims right at the boat, some people wish they would!

Molokini Island

Three miles off the coast of Maui, the dormant volcano called Molokini Island rises up from the ocean floor and breaks the surface, where its crater forms a crescent-shaped volcanic islet. Because the crescent acts like a breakwater to waves and currents, the islet is a sanctuary for marine life and a breathtaking scuba diving and snorkeling spot. It has been rated one of the world's top ten favorite dive sites, and it is unquestionably one of the world's most unusual.

Molokini is accessible only by boat—truly a voyage to a magic world. Slipping off the dive boat and into the cool water is like descending into an aquarium: the site is virtually free of soil runoff, and the crystal-clear water glows all the way down to the ocean floor, some three hundred feet below. The crater has three diving tiers: a 35-foot-deep plateau inside the crater basin for snorkelers, a wall sloping to 70 feet just beyond this plateau, and a sheer wall on the outside of the crater that plunges 350 feet. Schools of bright tropical fish whirl around and dart back and forth, obviously looking for a snack. Far below, manta rays swim gracefully by, undulating across the ocean bottom. The crater is a manta ray cleaning station, where the great rays take turns being groomed by cleaner wrasse. Divers who venture to the

A garden of colorful snorkels indicates the presence of underwater explorers at this divers' paradise.

back of the crater tell of close encounters with small white-tipped sharks, turtles, and moray eels.

Hawaiian legends say that Molokini was once a beautiful woman with the ability to turn into a *mo'o*, a dragon lizard. She dared to fall in love with a man fancied by Pele, the fiery volcano goddess—and nobody messed with Pele's men and got away with it. The jealous Pele simply cut her rival in two, transformed her into stone, and tossed her into the ocean. Her tail formed the crescent of Molokini, and her head landed on Mākena Beach, where it formed a cinder cone.

Ho'okipa Beach

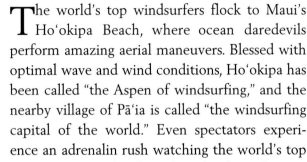

Strip off your clothes that are a nuisance in this mellow climate. Get in and wrestle with the sea; wing your heels with the skill and power that reside in you; bite the sea's breakers, master them, and ride upon their backs as a king should.

—Jack London

The world's top windsurfers flock to Maui's Ho'okipa Beach, where ocean daredevils perform amazing aerial maneuvers. Blessed with optimal wave and wind conditions, Ho'okipa has been called "the Aspen of windsurfing," and the nearby village of Pā'ia is called "the windsurfing capital of the world." Even spectators experience an adrenalin rush watching the world's top windsurfers, their bright sails taut, smash into waves head-on in order to gain "hang-time" up in the air.

The crashing surf also tempts board surfers forever in search of "the Big One." Since the wind isn't really at its peak until afternoon, board surfers mostly have the waves to themselves in the morning hours. Many of these leathery, tanned sportsmen are the original flower-children/surfers who dropped out of mainstream society at the dawn of the Age of Aquarius to settle in Pā'ia, vowing to surf until they dropped dead.

When giant winter waves soar seven stories high at "Jaws," the nearby ocean surf break, spectators line the cliffs and adjacent pineapple fields, clamoring for a glimpse of big-wave surfers far out at sea. The frightening height of the winter swells here has historically made Jaws a place for experts only, but the advent of tow-in surfing has changed that. Now, Ho'okipa is packed in wintertime with thrill-seekers yearning to ride Jaws' monster waves and win the $1,000-per-foot award offered by the surf company Billabong. (In 2004, the award reached the sum of $68,000!) Safety officials and seasoned big-wave surfers are looking for ways to deal with the seasonal onslaught of daredevil amateurs.

"The Challenge at Mānele" Golf Course

Carved from lava fields 150 feet above the crashing ocean, the magnificent "Challenge at Mānele" in Lāna'i beckons golfers from around the world. Every hole offers sweeping ocean views, and the dramatic terrain of plunging gorges and verdant ravines makes for a thrilling, target-style game. The Par 3, Number 12 "signature hole," which plays from a cliff above the surf, requires a demanding, 200-yard tee shot across the Pacific Ocean. Designed by all-time golf great Jack Nicklaus, the course rated #1— tied with the Lodge at Kō'ele, Lāna'i—in Golf Digest's "Top 10 Hawaiian Resorts for 2002," and was the Gold Medallist 2002 in Golf Magazine's rankings of "America's Best Resorts."

The island of Lāna'i has had many incarna- tions. For centuries, it was a desolate place said to be inhabited by man-eating ghosts and a powerful sorceress. Then, one day, it was redeemed by a young boy, Kaulula'au, known as the boy who "tricked the ghosts" and opened the island for human habitation. In 1922, James Dole turned the island into one big pineapple planta- tion, but the cost of labor rose so much that he sold out to entrepreneur David Murdoch, who took advantage of the island's distinct climates by building a mountain and a beach resort here. Pineapple pickers and young people who had left the island returned home to work for the resorts, and soon both the billionaires and backpackers one still sees today began frequenting Lāna'i, attracted by its relative isolation and lack of crowds.

Waikīkī

Waikīkī,
At night when shadows are falling,
I hear your rolling surf calling,
Calling and calling to me.

—from "Waikīkī," lyrics by Andrew Cummings

As the sun sets over the ocean of Waikīkī on the coast of Oʻahu, flaming tiki torches cast their glow over trees, flowers, and the outdoor restaurants of luxury hotels. Families on the beach, mai tai drinkers at Duke's Bar, and honeymooners on oceanfront lanais watch the indigo ocean intently, hoping to see the elusive green flash as the sun sinks below the horizon. As bronzed surfers rip through the waves and the colorful silhouettes of yachts bob up and down on the darkening sea, beams of soft light from the rising moon creep up from behind Diamond Head and stream down the slopes of the extinct volcano and across the ocean—the quintessential Waikīkī scene.

Archibald Menzies, in a journal of Vancouver's voyage in 1792, wrote:

> The view of this bay from the ship was truly delightful. The shore was bordered with low land, interspersed with groves of cocoanut palms, and . . . fertile plantations, such as we have already described, stretched back and mounted up the sides of the hills in various directions, forming a striking contrast with the high, steep and rugged mountains beyond them,

which occupied the interior parts of the island, and reared their peaked summits, apparently covered with wood, to a great elevation. These were again intersected by chasms and deep valleys whose verdant appearance indicated the fertility of their soil . . . In short, it was one of those interesting landscapes which the eye of a meditative mind could long contemplate with new-felt pleasure and move slowly over without wishing to quit its various and picturesque beauties.

In other words, Waikīkī was as seductive then as it is today. King Kamehameha had a compound here, as did future kings, and the beaches and waves of Waikīkī were a playground for royalty. Surfing was a sport enjoyed by all Hawaiians, but the waves at favored locations were *kapu* to commoners, and none would dare surf a wave claimed by a chief. Down through the ages, surfing continued as a popular tradition at the beach, and Waikīkī's beach boys—bronzed, strong, and friendly—became legends of the Waikīkī surf scene.

In the early twentieth century, one of these beach boys even brought surfing an international following. Duke Kahanamoku, an Olympic swimming champion and a Hawaiian icon, used to compete often in swimming meets on the East and West coasts of mainland America, and he would always take his surfboard with him and amaze onlookers as he rode the waves. When he went to Australia to compete in an international swim meet, however, he left his board at home. While there, he was stunned to discover that the Australians had never mastered board surfing, and so he promptly fashioned a surfboard out of a wooden plank and ripped down the waves of Freshwater Beach. Australians knew a good thing when they saw it, and the nation "down under" turned into a nation of surfing addicts. A statue of this great Hawaiian, known as the "Father of Modern Surfing," stands on Waikīkī Beach.

Today, Waikīkī is a round-the-clock beach party that attracts nearly five million visitors a year from all over the planet. Somehow, the beautiful beach still looks like a picture postcard, and beachgoers can still find their own sandy place under a rustling palm tree. At night, romantics linger on the warm sand or make their way along the wave-splashed seawalls on the promenade, entranced by flickering torches and drifting music. Right in the midst of it all, a strange little slice of ancient Hawai'i remains: four large wizard stones silently vibrating on the beach. The stones are said to possess the *mana*, spiritual power, of four hermaphrodite wizards renowned throughout Polynesia for their healing power.

Kailua Beach

Onreal (ahn reel) Unreal. Used to describe anything that gets your motor going, like somebody sexy, dynamite dope, or big waves. "Wow, unreal da sets, yeah?"
—"Pidgen to Da Max," Douglas Simonson

Powdery golden sand and an aquamarine ocean have earned Kailua Beach a place on "Dr. Beach's" list of the best beaches in the United States. The inviting, two-mile crescent of silky sand on Windward Oʻahu slopes gently into the deeper offshore water, providing a safe swimming area. After swimming, picnickers spread their beach mats on the green lawns of the beach park and watch the bright sails of windsurfers, hobie cats, and kiteboarders race across the bay before a backdrop of tiny offshore islands. In the late 1970s, Kailua Beach gained an international reputation as a windsurfing capital when surfers there fitted sails to surfboards and pioneered the California sport in Hawaiʻi. The beach is now home to Robbie Naish, world windsurfing champion.

Nearly a mile offshore, the twin islets of Mokulua beckon. These islets and the unbelievable green, turquoise, and dark blue hues of the ocean around them are so typical of a tropical dream that, a few years ago, a photo of the scene was used by a California advertising agency to advertise the islands of Australia. There was an uproar when people recognized the islands as part of Hawaiʻi and not Australia's Barrier Reef!

Waimea Bay

Men of the sun and the sea
Those men who ride mountains
Bend to the wind
Top to bottom, side to side
Looking for the ultimate ride.
　　　　　　　—Israel Kamakawiwoʻole

During the winter months, blue mountains of water thunder onto the beach at Waimea Bay, Oʻahu. When the giant ocean swells from the far Aleutians reach the steeply shelving shore at Waimea Bay, they turn into perfectly curved

Turtle swimming at North Shore, Oahu.

walls of terrifying water: some of the largest waves on earth. Here, the extreme sport of big wave surfing holds viewers enthralled.

At the entrance to the beach park, a plaque remembers Eddie Aikau, the first lifeguard at the bay and a Hawaiian hero. A popular bumper-sticker in Hawaii reads: Eddie Would Go. And Eddie did—saving thousands of lives in the dangerous surf when no one else would dare. As if that weren't enough, he also won many surfing competitions and stunned the crowds on the beach when he rode a forty-foot wave.

Eddie loved the ocean and was proud of his Hawaiian heritage. So, in 1978, he was thrilled to be invited to be one of the crew of the sixty-foot, double-hulled Polynesian voyaging ca-

North Shore surfing, O'ahu.

noe, *Hōkūle'a*, about to set sail for Tahiti. He even took along his surfboard, hoping to do some surfing once they arrived. As they sailed into the Moloka'i Channel, one of the most treacherous stretches of ocean on earth, a violent storm hit. The *Hōkūle'a* overturned, took on water, was lashed by gale force winds and 12-foot ocean swells, and eventually drifted out of shipping lanes. Hope seemed to be fading fast for the crewmembers, who could do nothing but cling to the hull.

Eddie decided to go for help. He volunteered to paddle his surfboard to the island of Lāna'i, some twelve miles to the east. A strong and fearless swimmer, he set off through the giant swells. The next morning, the crew of the *Hōkūle'a* was spotted by the pilot of an inter-island flight and rescued by helicopter. A massive search was launched for Eddie, but no trace of him was ever found.

When the waves at Waimea Bay reach heights of over twenty feet—nearly double that height when measured from the trough of the wave—the Eddie Aikau Big Waves Invitational kicks off. Thousands of spectators sit breathless on a beach drenched with sea spray, watching the men who ride mountains. And everybody there—spectators and surfers—remembers Eddie Aikau, the brave young man who gave his life for his friends. "I go down with the guys who are out," says Eddie Aikau Invitational big wave surfer Charlie Walker, quoted in Bruce Jenkins' North Shore Chronicles. "I go down with Eddie—every time I go out, I see him."

Hanauma Bay State Underwater Park

Snorkelers join thousands of tropical fish as they cruise the maze of underwater lava channels at East Oʻahu's curved Hanauma Bay, situated within a pair of volcanic craters. Seven thousand years ago, the strong current that begins far out at sea and crashes against Hanauma's cliffs broke through the rims of the extinct craters and took control of the area. The beach is protected by a shallow, fringing reef that brushes aside the ocean waves, leaving the waters of the bay tranquil and smooth.

Hawaiians have been coming to Hanauma Bay for over 1,000 years. Like many of the very best places, the bay was once *kapu*, meaning that only chiefs could go there. Queen Kaʻahumanu, an excellent surfer, came here by canoe to bathe in the tranquil waters. Hula festivals and *uma*, arm wrestling competitions, were held here, and the bay was a favorite royal fishing spot: with thousands of resident fish, a good catch would have been a certainty. Even after the *kapu* system was abolished, King Kamehameha II still considered Hanauma Bay his private fishing grounds.

Today, the entire bay has been set aside as an underwater park and conservation area. Wide-eyed behind their goggles, enraptured visitors watch striped convict tang swimming together in mob style, black and white Moorish idols zapping past, lionfish waving wing-like fins, and hundreds of other striped, spotted, squirting, and tentacled creatures doing what they do best. Keyhole, a large sandy break in the reef, is a particularly good place for skin diving and snorkeling. Hanauma Bay is extremely popular with tourists and frequently crowded, but swimmers can still have a private encounter with a turtle or trumpetfish in the early mornings and late afternoons.

Byodo-In Temple

All those who are unhappy in the world are so
As a result of their desire for their own happiness.
All those who are happy are so
As a result of their desire for the happiness of others.
          —A Guide to the Bodhisattva Way of Life 8.129

The ornate Byodo-In Temple in Windward Oʻahu is a replica of the 900-year-old architectural treasure located in Uji, Japan. The temple was constructed in 1968 to commemorate the 100th anniversary of Japanese immigration to the Hawaiian Islands. Before entering the temple, visitors first ring the three-ton brass Peace Bell to ensure they'll live a long life of peace and happiness. Inside, a nine-foot gold and lacquer Lotus Buddha imparts his eternal message of peace and harmony.

Byodo-In is the main feature of the Valley of the Temples, a memorial park in a spectacular setting. In this beautiful, peaceful place, peacocks stroll through the landscaped Japanese gardens, birds flit and chirp in the trees, and hundreds of bright, rainbow-colored carp (koi) dart around in the pond. According to the park caretaker, carp can live to be three hundred years old. A golden carp is worth thousands of dollars—which is why the pond doesn't have any!

The largest wooden Buddha carved in over 900 years, nine feet tall and covered in gold lacquer, dominates the interior of Byodo-In Temple.

Polynesian Cultural Center

Come, come, ye saints, no toil nor labor fear;
But with joy, wend your way.
Though hard to you this journey may appear,
Grace shall be as your day.
'Tis better far for us to strive
Our useless cares from us to drive;
Do this, and joy your hearts will swell
All is well! All is well!

—William Clayton, 1846

In 1864, Mormons settled in Lāʻie on Windward Oʻahu and established a sugar plantation. The 42-acre site is now the home of the Polynesian Cultural Center, a theme park that re-creates village life from seven Pacific island cultures: Samoa, New Zealand, Tahiti, Fiji, the Marquesas, Tonga, and Hawaiʻi. Each village features authentically built Polynesian huts and elaborate ceremonial houses furnished with weavings, tapa cloths, and carved utensils, and visitors can either walk from one to the next or catch a canoe ride in the tranquil lagoon.

Polynesian students from the adjacent Brigham Young University supplement their income by dressing in traditional fashion and giving hands-on craft demonstrations at the Polynesian Cultural Center. Visitors really feel like part of the village experience as they learn how to create cloth from the bark of mulberries, baskets from palm fronds, and poi from boiled taro roots. A canoe carver demonstrates his marvelous, age-old skills alongside beautifully handcrafted replicas of voyaging canoes from Fiji and Aotearoa.

In the afternoon, the colorful Pageant of Long Canoes glides through the lagoon with fifty Polynesian dancers acting out legends and myths of the Pacific. As stars fill the sky, visitors sample traditional Hawaiian foods at a luʻau and watch a Polynesian extravaganza with more than 100 performers at the park's indoor/outdoor amphitheater. For fast food Polynesian-style, lithe youths skim up tall palm trees to collect coconuts, which they hack open for a naturally fizzy drink.

The Polynesian Cultural Center started as an experiment. Local businessmen predicted it would fail, saying tourists would never travel to distant Lāʻie for a cultural presentation. Much to their surprise, hard work and the excellent performances of the young Polynesian students of Brigham Young University have turned the park into one of Oʻahu's top attractions, drawing around one million visitors a year.

Left: The Whare Runanga, or meeting house, is the focal point of the Maori Pa, or fortified compound, at the Polynesian Cultural Center. It sits facing the marae, or open area, and serves as the place where most presentations and important events in Maori tribal life occur.

Opposite: The most dominant feature of the Fijian village at the Polynesian Cultural Center is the bure kalou, *which literally means "spirit house" or temple In ancient times the traditional priest would go into such a temple to commune with the gods.*

Chinatown

Window of a sweet-smelling lei shop in Chinatown.

Early in the nineteenth century, Chinese plantation workers checked their fortune cookies and, lo and behold, they told them to quit the backbreaking work in the cane fields to become traders and businessmen in the area of Honolulu known today as Chinatown. This neighborhood, centered around King and Maunakea Streets, has seen many ups and downs. The worst of the downs occurred in 1900, when a fire that was deliberately set to burn out rats got out of control and burned down almost the whole district. Most of the streets' older buildings date from soon after that fire.

These days, Chinatown is a mix of the modern, the exotic, and the sleazy. Although the district is still the financial, commercial, and cultural center of O'ahu's Chinese community, businesses from the Philippines, Vietnam, Japan, and Korea have settled there as well. Like a small corner in a large Asian city, narrow, congested sidewalks bustle with fast-moving tiny ladies lugging big shopping bags. Exotic aromatic goods at small mom-and-pop shops burst out of open doors and onto the sidewalks. Hole-in-the-wall restaurants serve up spicy delights, noodles, and chop suey. Sweet-smelling lei shops overflow with orchids, tuberoses, and pīkake leis of intricately woven yellow, purple, and pink strands. Chinese herbalists promise cures for all ills with little bottles of herbs and magic potions. Pretty young prostitutes and jaded-looking pimps beckon to passersby while trying to avoid vigilant police. Open-air markets are crowded with hanging ducks, live chickens in crates, strange sea creatures wiggling on counters, and pigs' heads that gape at passersby. Visitors can find a cool oasis away from the crowd next to the impressive statue of Buddha inside the Kwan Yin Temple. Nearby, a gate featuring ferocious dragons guards the Izumo Taishakyo, a Japanese Shinto shrine.

The Chinatown Historical Society offers two free walking tours of Chinatown as well as of the nearby botanical delight, Foster Botanical Gardens. On the first Friday of each month, art lovers can pick up self-guiding maps from the downtown art galleries and check out the new hot spots of Honolulu's art world, including "The Arts at Mark's Garage" and the Contemporary Museum at First Hawaiian Bank. Theatergoers from the newly restored historic Hawai'i Theater chat animatedly around the fountain in the courtyard of the Eurasian eatery Indigo. As new and old mix together more and more each day, the image of 140-year-old Chinatown is being perpetually redefined.

University of Hawai'i at Mānoa

Leafy paths meander through the campus grounds of the University of Hawai'i, established in 1907 in green Mānoa Valley, Honolulu. This is one of the world's few campuses perpetually blessed by rainbows. It's no surprise, then, that the multi-cultural university draws students from all over the world. The university's East-West Center is one of the world's chief exchanges of Occidental and Oriental thought. The adjacent Thai Pavilion was a gift from the king of Thailand. Jefferson Hall is guarded by Chinese lions and has a serene Japanese garden with a stream and a teahouse called the Cottage of Tranquility.

A new Hawaiian Studies building is located alongside ancient taro terraces that have been brought alive again with shiny-leaved taro plants. The impressive new building's architecture reflects Hawaiian design, and its very existence is symbolic of the rise of the study of Hawaiian issues and the Hawaiian language. The growing desire among Hawaiians to regain their culture and identity is a movement that is advancing by leaps and bounds, and the University of Hawai'i is leading the way.

Honolulu Academy of Arts

The indoor/outdoor Honolulu Academy of Arts, with its sloping tile roof, columned veranda, and thick white stucco walls, is an appropriate combination of East and West. Chinese horses stand at the entrance, and Japanese gardens surround European-inspired cloisters. The academy's courtyards hold statues from the sixth century A.D. and an impressive Egyptian figure that dates to about 2500 B.C. The academy's art collections are almost equally divided between Western and Asian art. The Western art collection encompasses more than 15,000 works from Europe and the United States, from classical antiquity to contemporary art. The upstairs gallery holds a sizable collection of local artworks that document Hawai'i's history as seen through the eyes of its gifted artisans. The academy's Asian art collection consists of more than 16,000 works from China, Korea, Japan, the Philippines, Southeast Asia, and India. Galleries hold magnificent Korean ceramics, Chinese furniture, and Japanese wood block prints, including a large collection of wood block prints donated by author James Michener. A small gallery holds Islamic art from the collection of Doris Duke, and from this gallery tours lead visitors to Ms. Duke's Shangri La Estate near Kāhala, where even more intriguing Islamic and Southeast Asian art and furnishings collections are to be admired.

Films and concerts, often of an alternative nature, are shown in the adjacent Academy Theater, and the Pavilion Cafe is a pretty place for outdoor dining.

Limahuli Botanical Gardens

Kaua'i is called the "Garden Island," and Limahuli Botanical Gardens, located in Hā'ena, on the North Shore of Kaua'i, is just one of the island's many Gardens of Eden. Juliet Rice Wichman and her grandson, Chipper Wichman, donated the 17-acre gardens and the 985-acre preserve to the National Tropical Botanical Gardens Society. Today, their gift has become a living classroom blossoming with research, educational, and teaching programs.

The fertile soil of Limahuli, which means "turning hands," was first turned by the strong hands of the island's original Polynesian settlers. Many treasured species brought by canoe thousands of miles across the ocean and carefully tended by these first arrivals still thrive at Limahuli: taro plants, whose starchy roots were pounded into poi, the Polynesians' staple food; wauke, from which tapa cloth was made; and lena, used to make dye and medicine. In addition to these, the botanical gardens showcase all sorts of tropical plants, both ancient and modern. White hibiscus blooms in profusion, as does the small yellow alula.

The gardens are sheltered by the Nā Pali cliffs and Mount Makana (the alluring "Bali Hai" in the movie South Pacific). A trail through the gardens leads to an overlook of the green-swept valley and the waterfall that tumbles 1,000 feet over the cliff. Visitors can stroll the lower garden or take a longer hike to the higher reaches of the valley, but the vast interior of the valley is open only to botanists.

Allerton Gardens

In the beautiful Lāwaʻi Valley on the south shore of Kauaʻi, the 100-acre Allerton Gardens were once the summer vacation home of Hawaiʻi's Queen Emma, who planted the scarlet bougainvillea that tumbles down the cliff walls. Father and son Robert and John Gregg Allerton, members of the cattle-raising family that founded the National Bank of Chicago, purchased the estate in 1938. The Allertons were garden lovers, art connoisseurs, and landscape designers, and they traveled around the South Pacific and brought back living treasures to create the elaborate gardens. In addition to these still thriving species, the

gardens now hold the world's largest collection of native Hawaiian flora: some 270 species. When Hurricane Iniki roared through Kaua'i in September 1992, hundreds of native plants were wiped out, but great effort on the part of the gardeners to replace and propagate plants quickly returned the gardens to their former splendor.

The Lāwa'i River runs through the valley alongside Allerton Gardens, and pretty pools refresh wandering visitors. Enchanting "garden rooms" feature different flowers and plants, whimsical statues stand scattered about, and surprises like "dinosaur eggs" lie nestled in the great root buttresses of a Moreton Bay fig tree. These giant trees and all the other primordial vegetation of the surrounding valley were a backdrop for the movie *Jurassic Park*.

Kalalau Trail

On the north shore of Kauaʻi, the dragon-teeth ridges of the Nā Pali Mountains tower 3,000 feet above the narrow Kalalau Trail as it winds eleven strenuous miles from Kēʻē Beach to Kalalau Valley. More than a thousand years ago, early settlers of the islands carved the trail, now the premier hike in Kauaʻi and perhaps in the entire state. Kalalau's difficulty was rated by the Sierra Club as a nine out of ten.

Many people hike the first two miles of the trail to Hanakāpiʻai Beach. This moderately easy stretch leads through dripping glades of kukui and ohia trees and rewards the hiker with breathtakingly beautiful views of the fluted Nā Pali Coast and the blue lagoons of Kēʻē Beach far below. Hanakāpiʻai's thundering surf has fierce currents that are wild and dangerous—not a good place to swim. The beautiful beach is the perfect place for a picnic, however, with a shallow, pale-green lagoon and a tempting, bubbling stream. From the beach, a trail shaded by huge mango trees follows the stream inland to the roaring 300-foot Hanakāpiʻai Falls.

The trail from Hanakāpiʻai to Hanakoa makes a steady climb along windswept cliffs and through narrow gulches that end suddenly in sheer, long drops to the sea below. Icy waterfalls cascade into pools and streams bordered with ferns and fragrant yellow ginger. Below, a thick canopy of spiky pandanus and light-green kukui (candlenut) trees sways like a circus safety net between the ocean and the narrow trail—a jungle barrier that has saved many hikers who have lost their balance. This is Indiana Jones-type scenery: above, jagged, towering peaks pierce the clouds; below, the inviting ocean sparkles, far out of the reach of the sweating hiker. Ancient terraces—some still growing taro, the plant used to make the starchy Hawaiian poi—and stone platforms are proof that Hawaiians lived and farmed in the valley—man, they must've been in good shape! More recent, temporary residents

View of Kēʻē Beach from Kalalau Trail

149

View of the Nā Pali coastline from Kalalau Trail

were the stars and film crews of *King Kong*, *Raiders of the Lost Ark*, and *Jurassic Park*.

The trail continues upward, past ledges not recommended to anyone with acrophobia, down gullies and cliffs of crumbling brown shale, and then all the way up to the crest of a red hill overlooking Kalalau Valley, a dizzy thousand feet below. Sloping towards the golden beach and crashing ocean, the valley seems a vast natural amphitheater enclosed by sheer cliffs crowned with green gothic spires, its gorges of emerald sliced through by silver streams.

Today, the State of Hawai'i forbids backpackers from staying in the valley for more than five days. Considering how difficult it is to reach the valley in the first place, the law seems rather mean-spirited to nature-loving travelers, but it was introduced to protect the lush valley from becoming a haven for refugees from modern society. The difficult-to-reach Kalalau is also difficult to police, however, and some hippies and "die-in-the-wood" residents remain, happily living in caves and foraging for guava, papaya, poi, and pot in the valley's abundance of wild gardens.

Movie Making in Hawaiʻi

The Hawaiian Islands have served as the back-drop and even as the stars of many motion pictures. Island tour companies offer trips to out-of-the-way sites like Huleiʻa Stream in east Kauaʻi, where Indiana Jones fans can kayak up to the pool from Raiders of the Lost Ark, grab a vine, and swing across just like Harrison Ford. Many might even be more successful at it than Mr. Ford himself: word has it that he tried again and again to perfect his swing, but eventually had to have a stuntman do it. Other great movies filmed in Hawaiʻi are:

From Here To Eternity, Hālona Cove, East Oʻahu

One of the most famous kisses in movie history took place on the sandy shore of tiny Hālona Cove, East Oʻahu. As waves surged over Deborah Kerr and Burt Lancaster lying in a passionate embrace on the beach, Deborah Kerr murmured, "I never knew it could be like this." Almost thirty years later, the December 11, 1981 edition of *The Hollywood Reporter* declared this scene the most famous love scene in film history. Kerr commented, "All I remember is that after a full

Blow hole at Eternity Beach, Hālona Cove, East Oʻahu. The tiny beach was unnamed until the famously romantic scene in From Here to Eternity *was filmed there in 1953.*

Hālona Cove, East O'ahu, where Burt Lancaster and Deborah Kerr rolled in the sand for the 1953 film From Here to Eternity.

day's filming of the scene, with all that sand in my bathing suit, my skin was rubbed raw!" The cove is now called "Eternity Beach." Some cynics call the secluded, romantic spot "Maternity Beach."

Blue Hawaii, Wailua, Kaua'i

Come with me
While the moon is on the sea,
The night is young
And so are we.
Dreams come true
In blue Hawai'i
And mine could all come true
This magic night of nights with you.
  —from *Blue Hawai'i*, lyrics by Leo Robin
and Ralph Rainger

Blue Hawaii introduced a generation of Americans to the beautiful sights of Hawai'i. In the movie, Chad (Elvis Presley) tells his father that tourism is the future of the islands. The movie itself made this something of a self-fulfilling prophecy: once the King of Rock 'n Roll had set foot there, the Hawaiian Islands became irresistible. Elvis and his silver-screen bride floated in a lei-bedecked canoe down a lagoon at Coco Palms Resort, Kaua'i. The resort was later severely damaged in Hurricane Iniki, but its namesake palm trees still sway just as they did when the happy couple was there. The lilting Hawaiian Wedding Song from the movie still sets the mood at many an island wedding; it's even possible to hold a *Blue Hawaii* wedding on the platform of the very same outrigger canoe as did the King himself.

South Pacific, Lumaha'i Beach, Kaua'i

Bali Ha'i may call you,
Any night, any day,
In your heart, you'll hear it call you,
Come away…come away.
  —from *South Pacific*, lyrics and music by
Rodgers and Hammerstein

153

A thatched-roof hut at Wailua, Kaua'i, where scenes for the movie Blue Hawaii *were filmed in 1961.*

Kaua'i was the perfect location for the musical *South Pacific*, based on James Michener's novel *Tales of the South Pacific*. Michener's fantastical island of Bali Ha'i was a composite of numerous scenic places, including pinnacled Mount Makana, lush Allerton Gardens, and Hā'ena Beach, which became the Bali Ha'i Village for filming. Scenes set at Rossano Brazzi's plantation were filmed at Hanalei Bay. Golden Lumaha'i Beach featured as the nurses' beach, where Mitzi Gaynor sang, "I'm Gonna Wash That Man Right Out of My Hair." Actual Marine and Navy maneuvers near Barking Sands on the west coast of Kaua'i were filmed for the war sequence. Movie buffs can rent a kayak to row up Kīlauea River and slide down the small waterfall, as did the frolicking young actress who played Bloody Mary's Tonkinese daughter, Liat.

Jurassic Park, Nā Pali Coast, Kaua'i
The Land Cruisers had stopped at the rise of a hill. They overlooked a forested area sloping down

Wailua, Kaua'i, where Elvis' character, Chad, was married on a canoe floating in a lagoon in the 1961 film Blue Hawaii.

to the edge of the lagoon. The sun was falling to the west, sinking into a misty horizon. The whole landscape of Jurassic Park was bathed in soft light, with lengthening shadows. The surface of the lagoon rippled in pink crescents. Farther south, they saw the graceful necks of the apatosaurs, standing at the water's edge, their bodies mirrored in the moving surface. It was quiet, except for the soft drone of cicadas. As they stared out at that landscape, it was possible to believe that they really had been transported millions of years back in time to a vanished world.

"It works, doesn't it?" they heard Ed Regis say, over the intercom. "I like to come here sometimes, in the evening. And just sit."

Grant was unimpressed. "Where is T- rex?"
—from *Jurassic Park*, Michael Crichton

Lumaha'i Beach, Kaua'i, where Mitzi Gaynor sang, "I'm Gonna Wash That Man Right Out of My Hair" in the 1958 filming of South Pacific.

Lumahaʻi Beach, Kauaʻi, used as the nurses' beach in the 1958 filming of South Pacific.

The misty valleys, tangled rain forest, and mountain ramparts of the island of Kauaʻi provided the stage for one of the most popular films ever, *Jurassic Park*. The Steven Spielberg film, adapted from the book by Michael Crichton, grossed just over $900 million world-wide and received three Academy Awards, including Best Visual Effects. Filming locations included Allerton Gardens, where dinosaur eggs can still be seen nestled in the roots of a giant ficus tree. Tour guides offer 4-wheel-drive trips to rainbow-misted Manawaiopuna Falls near Hanapepe Valley, Hanapepe Falls, and Blue Hole, Wailua, with a hike up a riverbed to the base of Mount Waiʻaleʻale's crater. As the Olokele Valley can be reached only by air, the production crew built a helipad there.

Jurassic Park began principal photography on the island on August 24, 1992. But three weeks into filming, a real life drama occurred: Hurricane Iniki, with winds of 120 miles per hour, headed straight for Kauaʻi. By afternoon, it became apparent that the hurricane was going to slam right into the island. Movie crews and stars filled the bathtubs with drinking water and packed their belongings, then huddled together with other hotel guests in the ballroom of the Westin Hotel. When water flooded one end of

Left: Nā Pali Coast, Kauaʻi, where the cast and crew of Jurassic Park *were hit hard by Hurricane Iniki during the 1992 filming.*

Opposite: The Nā Pali Coast on the island of Kauaʻi, where Steven Spielberg filmed Jurassic Park *in 1992.*

the ballroom, everybody moved to the other side. Outside, the furious hurricane rumbled and roared across the island. By evening, Kauaʻi was flattened, with no power, electricity, or working phone on the island, hence no communication with the outside world. There was also no way of leaving: the runway and buildings at the airport were filled with palms, sand, and water, and every helicopter was tipped on its side. Kauaʻi was devastated, with damages estimated at some $500 million.

It took days before the 130-member crew could be evacuated from the island. (But hey, at least they went home with some really great footage for a sequel!) Obviously, all the movie sets were smashed to bits. Fortunately for the movie's producers, *Jurassic Park* had only one day's filming to complete. For that last day, some of the crew returned from Hollywood to Oʻahu, where they filmed the dinosaurs galloping across the green fields of Kualoa Ranch.

Index